EVERLASTING LOVE

DEVOTIONAL SERMONS

by

REV. MURDOCH CAMPBELL, M.A.

"But the path of the just is as the shining light, that shineth more and more unto the perfect day" (Pro. 4, v. 18).

Published by

THE KNOX PRESS, 15 NORTH BANK STREET
THE MOUND, EDINBURGH, 1.

Printed by

JOHN G. ECCLES
Henderson Road, Longman
Inverness

Alison MacDonald.

Dec. 1968

Alison MacDonald.

Dec. 1968

EVERLASTING LOVE

PREFACE

These sermons, which had been typed by one or two friends, are printed, more or less, as they were preached. When a friend, who is also a member of the Knox Press Publications, asked me some time ago if I had any available material for printing, I handed him — with some measure of hesitation — these sermons. This I did in the hope that, through the Lord's blessing, they might be a means of help and comfort to His people. The sermons are, perhaps, more devotional and experimental than theological or expository. They are also, I hope, lucid and simple enough to be understood by all who may read them.

ORDER OF SERMONS

I

"GOD'S EVERLASTING LOVE"

"The Lord hath appeared unto me of old saying, "Yea, I have loved thee with an everlasting love; therefore with loving kindness have I drawn thee." (Jer. 31 : 3).

When these words were first spoken by the prophet, God was laying many and heavy chastisements on His people for their sins. But lest their spirits should fail under their afflictions, and lest they should be tempted to think that the Lord had forgotten to be gracious, He sends them a reassuring word of unspeakable consolation. It was not a word spoken to them only, but is meant for all the people of God in every age. In seeking to understand something of the significance and implications of these inconceivably precious words let us consider:

I. The Nature of God's Love

It is "everlasting". That word "everlasting" means something which, like a river, is ever flowing. Under this figure we may say that this love had its rise and wellspring in the heart and sovereign will of God. It is the river of His "good pleasure", the streams of which make glad the city of God both in Heaven and on earth. Unlike the love of God, our love to Him has a beginning in time, though it shall have no end. His love flows on through eternal ages without a beginning or an end. "Unto Him who **loves** us." The present tense in this phrase implies a beginningless and endless continuity.

There are three Persons in the Godhead, but only, as Augustine reminds us, **una mens,** or one mind. Therefore His love also is one. It is the love of the Triune God. This love, however, has its several manifestations and its different exercises. We speak, for example, of the electing love of the Father, the redeeming love of the Son, and the sanctifying love of the Holy Ghost. "God is love", and His love is, therefore, like Himself. It is infinite, eternal, unchangeable and unsearchable. It is everlasting in its duration. It is infinite, or like a sea without a shore. It is unchangeable or like an ocean which is always at full tide. It is unfathomable in its depth, and unsearchable in the mystery of its grace and choice. Paul once prayed that the new-born Church at Ephesus might be able to know, "with all the saints what is the breadth, and length, and depth, and height of the love of Christ which passeth knowledge." He told them of this life-giving plenitude, out of which they might drink, that they also "might be filled with the fullness of God."

It was this everlasting love which was in the heart of God that gave full exercise to all His glorious attributes in the salvation of His Church. All His gifts and blessings may also be traced to His love. Both Christ and the Holy Spirit, with the countless blessings associated with each, are the gifts of His love. "God so loved the world that He gave His only begotten Son," And God "who spared not his own Son but delivered Him up for us all, how shall He not with Him also freely give us all things?"

Again God's love is necessarily sovereign. It arose spontaneously in Himself "according to the good pleasure of His will" and without any worthiness on our side. There was nothing in our persons or in our works to draw this love towards us. There was, on the other hand, everything to repel. He loved us, not for what we were, but in spite of what we were. Paul could never forget the stupendous miracle of Christ's sovereign love to himself. He who raged against and persecuted the infant Church, and who spoke of himself as "the chief of sinners", marvelled that the Son of God should love him and give Himself for him. It was he who afterwards wrote of how "the kindness and love of God appeared to men, not by works of righteousness which we have done but according to His mercy He saved us." (Titus 3).

This is also a love which is intimately personal. "I have loved thee." He loves each of His people as He loves all. In conscious possession of Christ's love and promise every Christian may say: "My Beloved is mine." To many believers God communicates this sweet secret — that they were the subjects of His love from all eternity. In the manifestation and assurance of His love to the soul there is an all-absorbing apprehension of Christ as the One who is fairer than the sons of men, and of the glory of His finished work.

II. The way in which His Love was revealed

It was revealed "of old". He loved us "from afar". So the word might be translated. It embraces not only the idea of duration but also of distance. God, in the dignity of His Being, is an infinite distance from all the creatures whether in Heaven or on earth. He is far above all. The highest angel before the throne is, in point of being, an immeasurable distance from Him who dwells in light which is inaccessible, and who is infinite in

Himself. But who can measure the moral and spiritual distance between God and the sinner? Modern scientists labour, as it were, in the grip of mathematics as they try to give expression to the vast inconceivable distances between the various stars in that part of the universe which is under the observation of their limited perception. These are, however, mere fractions of distance compared to the distance between the Throne of Glory in the highest Heaven and "the far country" where the sinner is. That distance was so great that only God's love and wisdom, in the Person of His dear Son, could ever span it. "The Lord is high above all nations, and His glory above the heavens. Who is like unto the Lord our God who dwells on high. Who humbleth Himself to behold the things which are in heaven and in earth." "He raiseth up the poor out of the dust, and the needy out of the dunghill." (Ps. 113). How wonderful it is that God should look in such a way "on the base things of the world and on the things which are despised."

If light travels far and fast how much more does the love of God! Distance and duration are, indeed, two aspects of His marvellous love. When the prophet uses the words "of old" he also brings the idea of duration within historical time. The word may even express God's first manifestation of His love to his own soul. We think, however, that he is speaking on behalf of the Church of God in every age. This love which was in God from everlasting was revealed to man in the very morning of Time. Think of Adam and Eve trying to hide themselves among the trees of the garden. At that solemn hour God sought them, and having pronounced the dread sentence which their sin, and ours in them, called forth, He there and then opened for them a door of hope. Mercy shone through the thick darkness, and the terrors of His just curse were pierced through by beams of love eternal. From the lips of God fell that word which contained the promise of a Redeemer. "The seed of the woman" would come to bruise the serpent's head. Within that unspeakably precious word were hid those great depths and the mystery of that divine grace which the ages of eternity cannot fully declare. (Ps. 106 : 2). From that hour drops began to fall from Heaven, and the finger of God began to draw aside the curtain till, in the fulness of the times, there was a real and final manifestation of His love and glory in the gift and work of His own eternal Son. But what, we may ask, are

III. **The Evidence and Characteristics of His Love**

A primary characteristic of love is that **it seeks nearness to its subjects.** We naturally seek nearness to those whom we love. And

Christ came near to the Church in the everlasting council of peace. He then undertook to be her Husband and Saviour. As it is customary among men for the father "to give away" his daughter on the day of her marriage, so in the transactions of eternity, when the Son consented to redeem His people, God the Father gave them to the Son in an indissoluble covenant. "Thine they were and thou gavest them me." "He that hath the Bride is the Bridegroom." Nearer He could not come. This is the most solemn and the most mysterious relationship known to man. "This", says Paul, "is a great mystery, but I speak concerning Christ and the Church." (Eph. 5 : 32).

He came near to them in another way. There is a lovely law in nature, whereby all the creatures dwell together "after their kind". This wonderful law nature observes in the most impressive way. The Great Author of this law of kinship imparted sanctity and honour to it when He united our nature to His own Person for ever. Thereby He became what He was not till then — He became Man. "Forasmuch then as the children are made partakers of flesh and blood, He also Himself likewise took part of the same." (Heb. 2). He married our nature that He might come near to us and dwell with us, and that He might be a true Husband to us in all love and tenderness. God the Father prepared a body for Him, and the Spirit conceived it in the womb of the Virgin. He took our nature without its sin, and yet with its sinless infirmities — that He might enter into our trials, temptations and sorrows, and that in a real, personal and experimental sense His love and pity might flow to all His suffering people to the end of time. The Church, indeed, is the weaker vessel, but her exalted Lord is still touched with a feeling of her infirmity.

He took our nature also that He might destroy the sin which had destroyed us, and "him who had the power of death, that is, the devil". How wonderful to think that from all eternity our Lord joyously anticipated the day when, as "a man of sorrows" He should inhabit the earth, and in their nature and likeness tabernacle with men in order that He might deliver them out of the hand of Satan who had led them captive in their fall!

Another characteristic of Christ's love was **its willingness to suffer** for those on whom it rests. Our Lord found His people ready to perish for ever in the cruel, unrelenting grasp of sin and death. They had the sentence of death in themselves. They came to know also that God's justice, in perfect righteousness, was, like an avenging sword, ready to slay them. They heard the accusing voice of the Holy Law — whose just demands are that we should perfectly love the Lord and one another — speaking against their sins. The voice from the mountain which is shrouded in unrelieved darkness they heard like thunder reverberating through a guilty conscience. "Cursed is every one that continueth not in all the works of the Law to do them." But for the joy set before Him Christ faced all the spiritual and physical agonies, all the shame and reproach, all the wrath, and all the heavy and unavoidable afflictions which their sins deserved. "He who knew no sin was made sin for us." The whole weight of our iniquities with all the sorrows and sicknesses which they bore, He took upon Himself. Our sins, which were imputed to Him, became His own. In love He died our death. "For the transgression of my people was He smitten." This He did, that His perfect righteousness and merit, might, in being imputed to us, render us for ever acceptable to God. O, what love moved Him to do all this. "Christ loved the Church and gave Himself for it . . . that He might present it to Himself a glorious Church without spot or wrinkle or any such thing." And in the day of her final presentation to Him in Heaven, when in His righteousness and image she shall appear in all the wonder of eternal youth and loveliness, He shall rejoice over her as a young man rejoiceth over his bride.

As love is willing to suffer **it is also willing to give.** Christ possesses unsearchable riches. As God's only and eternally begotten Son He is the "Heir of all things". The Father gave all things into His hand. As the Mediator of the New Covenant God gave Him the fulness of the Spirit and all the treasures of His wisdom and grace. The blessing is "on the head of Joseph and top of the head of him who was separated from His brethren." But, in a deed of testament, Christ gave His riches away! That testament became valid when He died. "Ye know the grace of our Lord Jesus Christ, how though he was rich, yet for our sakes he became poor that ye through his poverty might be rich." These unsearchable and inexhaustible riches are administered in the Gospel now, and will be administered throughout endless ages in the kingdom of glory. This is love indeed; and this is good news for the poor in Zion. God is able to supply all our needs "according to his riches in glory by Jesus Christ." Throughout eternity His people shall be led to make new discoveries of the wonderful love "which passeth knowledge". Happy are all they whose prayer is:

"Remember me, Lord with that love,
Which thou to thine dost bear,
With thy salvation, O my God,
To visit me draw near."   (Ps. 106).
Another blessed characteristic of this love is **its irresistible power.**

"And with loving kindness have I drawn thee." Christ found His people dead in trespasses and sin; but in a day of His power He quickened them and called them effectually to Himself. He passed by them and said, "Live", and He made their time "a time of love". He drew them out of a state of death and darkness "with the cords of love and with the bands of a man." They saw His love in dying for them on the Cross. This, especially, is what melted their heart, drew them into His bosom, and made them weep at His feet. "I if I be lifted up from the earth will draw all men unto me." From this love they can never be separated; for "who shall separate us from the love of Christ?" From that day a prayer was born in their heart: "Draw me and we will run after thee." Those who have His love in their soul shall be enabled to persevere to the end of their pilgrimage journey. "Love never faileth." Many waters cannot quench it. It is stronger than death and jealous as the grave. Let me very briefly and in conclusion mention:

IV. **Some of the marks which belong to those who know this love.**

There is one place where all God's people meet. They meet within the great declaration— "We love Him who first loved us." This is, therefore, a reciprocating love. All whom Christ loved will come to love Christ. We know, of course, that there are degrees of this love within the Church of God, but, in this world, none can love Him in the measure in which He deserves. No, nor yet throughout eternity.

Now, the love of Christ in the heart is not a mere emotion. It is certainly something which lodges in our heart, but which has also its outward manifestation in the life of all His people. To love Christ is to obey Him. "If ye love me keep my commandments." And to His own His commandment is not grievous but joyous. God's child loves God's will as it is revealed in His Word, and, like David, when he or she sees God's law disparaged and trampled under foot of men, "rivers of waters run down their eyes".

Those who love Christ would serve Christ. In this our own day when "the harvest truly is plenteous and the labourers are few" how we ought to exert ourselves in His service! But with iniquity abounding on all sides the love of many has waxed cold. O! that we might in this day of small things and during life's brief hour, show our love to Him by doing what we can, and especially by wrestling with Him in secret that His kingdom may come and that the kingdom of darkness might be destroyed.

His people not only serve Him but they also suffer for Him. "Unto you it is given on behalf of Christ not only to believe on Him but also to suffer for His sake." The page of history tells us of the physical sufferings of the Church in other days. To her, literally speaking, His love was better than life. Many lay down their lives for their love to Him. But we believe that the greatest trials of God's people are often inward, and proceed from their conflicts with sin and Satan. A great Divine once wrote a letter to a friend in which he said that in the measure in which we love God in the same measure will Satan hate us. "For thus," he said, "is the nature of the love of God, according to the measure of it in the heart the most fiery and envenomed darts of Satan will pierce through our spirits tempting us to despise Him whose glory we account preferable to all creation." But His love in our heart "endures all things". If we are His, very soon we shall be drawn beyond the reach of all that distresses us here.

Then, in that fair world beyond the skies, we shall sing together His praise

"But as for me I with my mouth
Will greatly praise the Lord,
And I among the multitude
His praises will record."   (Ps. 109).

II

" THE GOD OF BETHEL "

" I am the God of Bethel." — Gen. 31:13.

About twenty years had elapsed in the life of Jacob between the wonderful night at Bethel and this new manifestation of the Lord mentioned in our text. The Lord, in giving this fresh disclosure of Himself to Jacob, commanded him, at the same time, to leave Laban's house in Padan-aram. By this gracious and, we believe, longed for hour of blessing, Jacob made a deeper discovery of the love and faithfulness of God. The name — "The God of Bethel" — by which the Lord made Himself known to him would have brought back endearing and solemn memories of other days. This, indeed, is one of the divine names which cannot fail to touch a tender cord in the hearts of many of the Lord's people. "The God of Bethel". Sweet beyond words is His name! What does this Name mean in the experience of those who are heirs of salvation? Might we not say at the beginning of our remarks that the God of Bethel is:—

I. **A Prayer Answering God:** In another chapter Jacob speaks of Him as "The God who answered me in the day of my distress, and was with me in the way which I went". We believe that by the day of his distress he meant not only his night of wrestling with God at Peniel, but also that wonderful morning at Bethel. Let us for a moment envisage that day when Jacob bade a fond, if sad, farewell to his father and mother. Then he moved on toward an unknown country. As the shades of night began to fall, and the stars began to appear in the silent sky above him, a sense of loneliness, if not of fear, would have touched his heart. Then, in weariness, he laid him down and slept. Was there a prayer on his lips as he closed his eyes? We believe there was. It might have been, in effect, the words of the Psalmist: "When my father and my mother forsake me, then the Lord will take me up". Whatever prayer was articulate within his spirit God heard it, for he awoke out of sleep conscious that the Lord was beside him. The awe of the Eternal was upon his soul. God's presence and love filled his heart. "The Lord is in this place". The One who is with His people in every age and in all their trials was near him.

A remarkable thing about Jacob's experience was that he knew who was beside him. It was not something that he had never known before. He did not say, "What is this, and whose Presence do I feel? This is all strange to me". No. "This", he said, "is none other but the house of God and this is the gate of Heaven." Whatever other views may be held by good men on this subject does not this prove that Jacob had communion with the Lord before this hour and that he was already in a state of grace? We think it does. The words which are used to describe him as a young man in his fathers' house are, indeed, the same as are used with regard to Job of whom the Lord speaks as "a perfect man". Long before this hour, therefore, Jacob was a "pious" or a "perfect man dwelling in tents". But at Bethel his soul enjoyed a new blessing. The dew of Hermon descended upon his soul. He enjoyed much nearness to the Angel of the Covenant. God's voice and Presence became more real to him than ever before. He moved deeper into the dimensions of eternity. Such seasons of unusual nearness to the Lord may be rare in the lives of many of God's people. Their days of heaven upon earth, though few and far between, provide them with memories which are precious beyond words. This, we believe, was a morning which Jacob shall remember through everlasting ages.

From this place of bliss, and deep communion with God, Jacob came to the land of his affliction. For twenty years he endured many trials and deceptions under the cruel hand of Laban. His soul also might have pined for a new blessing and for more nearness to the Lord. Bethel became a wistful memory. Would he ever again stand in the suburbs of Heaven as he did then, and hear that much-loved voice and enjoy a similar season of communion with the Holy One? Ah, dear friends, are there not seasons in our own life when we recall the years of His right hand — the season of our first love — and when with the Psalmist we also say:

"How long wilt Thou forget me, Lord,
 Shall it for ever be?
 O how long shall it be that Thou
 Wilt hide Thy face from me?"

Some of us echo the words of the godly Cowper when he penned the words:

"Where is the blessedness I knew
 When first I saw the Lord?
 Where is the soul refreshing view
 Of Jesus and His Word?"

But those who know the way to the Throne of Grace, and who know the Lord as a prayer-answering God know also that the

God of Bethel is:

II. **A Covenant Keeping God.** "He shall perform the truth to Jacob and the mercy to Abraham".

And true to His promise He appeared to Jacob the second time. There was indeed, a sense in which He was as near to Jacob over his long period of exile as He was on that memorable morning at Bethel. Not consciously, but in His promise and providential care. On his death bed he spoke solemnly of the Angel who fed him all his days. He could speak of Him also as the One who led and kept him throughout his earthly pilgrimage and amid the many dangers to which, in this life, he was exposed. The life of every believer is, in retrospect, a witness to God's covenant care and love. He watches over us night and day. He never slumbers nor sleeps. All the saints are in His hand. While we may sometimes complain of His silence we know that He is ever at our right hand. "I will never leave thee nor forsake thee." At the end of his life Jacob could see how true God was to His promise. "And behold I am with thee, and will keep thee in all places whither thou goest, and will bring thee again into this land; for I will not leave thee, until I have done that which I have spoken to thee of." It is interesting to note that this covenant also embraced Jacob's seed. One of the great miracles of history is seen in the way in which God has preserved in His providence "the seed of Jacob". Let us pray that the day may soon come when, by the outpouring of God's Spirit, they shall look upon Him whom they have pierced and disowned, and mourn.

There is a remarkable incident recorded in this chapter. It was in the heart of Laban to do Jacob harm. But we read how God appeared to him in a dream and warned him of the consequence of doing His prophet any harm. Truly God moves in a mysterious way. He can be terrible to those who would touch the apple of His eye. We read in the Psalm how, in the days of Abraham and Isaac, God did appear to mighty kings and warned them against touching His anointed. This, as Matthew Henry and others remind us, He did in dreams or visions. Little do the people of God know how they are kept from those, in hell and on earth, who would devour them. His covenant faithfulness is a bulwark between us and all our enemies. "This God is our God for ever and ever. He will be our Guide even unto death". But, pre-eminently, the God of Bethel is:

III. **The God of Revelation.** Jacob's dream was, above all, a supernatural disclosure of God's way of salvation. It was a type of Him who is the only Mediator between God and man. Christ is God's "Daysman" whose hand, in the words of Job, rest on

God and on His people. He alone unites Heaven and earth. If the one end of His ladder rests on the earth, the other end reaches into the highest heaven. This lovely, mystic vision brings before us Christ, both in His Person as the God-man and in His state of humiliation and exaltation. When Nathanael stood before Him He uttered the words which prove that it was He who was so gloriously typified in this heavenly dream. "Hereafter ye shall see heaven open, and the angels of God ascending and descending upon the Son of Man." When our Lord spoke these words He was here among us in our nature and in the likeness of sinful flesh. The eternal and personal Word became incarnate. He took bone of our bone and flesh of our flesh. He who was, in the sinless infirmity of our nature, in the bosom of a woman — unable to walk and unable to speak — was at the same time, as God's Eternal Son, in the bosom of the Father. Great, indeed, is the mystery of Godliness. And the great end for which He became incarnate was that He might die for us. The way to Heaven, therefore, begins at the Cross of Calvary. At the place where He died we begin, by faith in His blood, by our reconciliation to God and our regeneration by His Spirit, to set out on that heavenly journey that ends within the portals of everlasting bliss. The innumerable company of angels who minister to the Church of God on Mount Zion are with us here because He also inhabited this earth. As no angel could appear on earth apart from His mediation and apart from the satisfaction which God in His law and justice received through His finished work, no sinner, on the other hand, is accepted of God and made heir of eternal glory in Heaven but through His death. It was, therefore, Christ the Angel of the Covenant who spoke to and was with Jacob in his dream, as it was He who was also there in the type. Christ is all and in all.

This is the place where all the people of God meet. The principal witness of the Holy Spirit in the written Word has to do with the sufferings of Christ and the glory that should follow. They are a people who are enlightened in the knowledge of Christ by the Holy Spirit. They know that before any of the elect of God, from Abel to the last of His people, could stand on the threshold of Heaven, Christ must stand on the earth. Our Lord pronounced Simon Peter a blessed man because God the Father, by the Holy Spirit, revealed to him that He who walked among men, without visible glory, was the Eternal Son of God, the Messiah and the Redeemer of His people. It is in and by the written Word that we see the glory of the Incarnate Word.

The two who were on the way to Emmaus, when the Lord

opened to them the Scriptures, sow in the word the mystery of godliness, God manifest in the flesh. How sweetly does His own description of Himself coincide with the view that His people enjoy of Him through the enlightenment of His Spirit. "I", He says, "am the rose of Sharon and the lily of the valleys." He who as God dwelt in the Sharon of the heavenly world was found in the valley of humiliation. He was in Heaven and on earth at the same time. His humiliation, sufferings and glory were also before the eyes of His Church when she exclaimed: "My beloved is white and ruddy, the chiefest among ten thousand." He came where we are that we might be where He is. "Father I will that they whom thou hast given me be with me where I am, that they may behold my glory." He tabernacled with us that we might, through His death and exaltation, dwell in His presence for ever.

And, beloved, are there not rare hours in our life when in our affections, desires and enjoyments we seem to be in another and better world? At such times we say, "Lord, it is good for us to be here". But here we have but the tabernacle of a wayfaring man. Clouds take Him out of our sight. The fond vision fades; for the just must live my faith. In Heaven shall our Bethel be permanent — and not till then. "And ye now therefore have sorrow; but I will see you again and your heart shall rejoice and your joy no man taketh from you." Peter speaks of the time when he, and the two other apostles, were with Christ on the holy mount, where they saw the glory of Zion's King and heard the voice from the most excellent glory which said, "This is my beloved Son in whom I am well pleased." But this great enjoyment he subordinates to the faith of the Church in God's word of promise. "We have also a more sure word of prophecy; whereunto ye do well that ye take heed, as unto a light that shineth in a dark place until the day dawn, and the day star arise in your hearts." God's word of promise stayed with Jacob after the lovely vision and the blissful presence were withdrawn. And in that word he trusted to the end. There are times when the Beloved withdraws Himself, but His word stays with us both in sunshine and cloud. This is our comfort in our affliction, for by His word are we kept and revived. Let us observe that the God of Bethel is also:

IV. **The God of Holiness.** We read that when Jacob awoke out of sleep he exclaimed: "How dreadful is this place." The awe of the Eternal rested on his spirit. At that moment something which has no parallel in human experience invaded his consciousness and touched his life. There he bowed his head, for he felt himself in the presence of a God infinitely holy. The nearer we come to God, or the nearer He comes to us, the more we realise our own sinfulness and insignificance. Therefore the deeper becomes our humility. This is what we see in the Scriptures. When God revealed to Job a little of His glory he bowed his head and said, "I have heard of thee by the hearing of the ear; but now mine eye seeth thee. Wherefore I abhor myself, and repent in dust and ashes." The same was true of God's prophet when in the temple he had a glimpse of the awesome majesty of the Triune God. "Woe is me, for I am undone . . . for mine eyes have seen the King, the Lord of hosts." Daniel was a man greatly beloved of God, but a man whose "comeliness was turned into corruption" when a ray of the divine glory was let fall on his spirit. Similar instances are before us in the New Testament when men like Peter, Paul and the apostle John shrank before the glory of Him who is the First and the Last. This holy humility shall stay with us throughout eternity in God's loving but awesome presence. "God is greatly to be feared in the assembly of the saints, and to be had in reverence of all them that are about him."

The dark fear which is in the heart of devils and evil men in relation to God is infinitely remote from the holy fear which lodges in the heart of God's child. The one has its roots in hatred toward Him and the other has its roots in holy love. The one would destroy God, and seeks separation and concealment from Him. The other embraces Him and is ever seeking greater nearness to Him and a greater holiness of life. The lost shall be eternally trying, in abject terror, to get away from His frown and presence. The redeemed know that the joy of Heaven has its source in the light of His countenance. The one says: "Depart from us, for we desire not the knowledge of thy ways." The other says "In thy presence is fulness of joy; at thy right hand there are pleasures for evermore." The God, therefore, in whose presence Jacob was afraid was, on the other hand, the Beloved of His soul. Deep reverence and holy love to God are kindred graces.

It was this apprehension of the holiness of God that led Jacob to separate himself from every species of idolatry, and which made him plead with his household to put away their strange gods and to purify themselves from the defilements of their idols. The God of Bethel had spoken to him again, demanding a deeper consecration of his life. He knew that he was in the presence of a "jealous" God to whom sin in every shape and form was a loathsome thing and the cause of alienating the affections of His people from Himself. And especially in our worship of His name is our sin in this respect most heinous.

Today, and within the visible Church, many have made a God in their own image and on their own level. The complacent and almost blasphemous irreverence with which graceless men address, and speak of, God is the evidence that they are as ignorant of Him as they are of themselves. This holy awe or dread has never touched their spirits. If it had they would say with others: "God be merciful to me a sinner."

But, perhaps, the sweetest thought that we can derive from these words is that the God of Bethel is:

V. **An Intimately Personal God.** "The God of Bethel" is also "The God of Jacob". How wonderfully do these words dovetail into one another. This is His name, and this is His memorial for ever. The Lord loves all His people equally, but each one makes a personal discovery of His love and care as if — in the words of Augustine — He loved no one but ourselves. The words, "My Lord and my God" have often, in moments of unusual nearness to the Christ, dropped like honey from the lips of Christ's spouse. "My beloved is mine, and I am His." This personal sense of possession and enjoyment shall remain with each and all of His people for ever and ever.

Is it not also true that each of us has his or her own personal and deeply valued spiritual experiences? We remember, like Jacob, places and seasons where and when the Lord refreshed our souls with a deep sense of His Presence. Sometimes in the secret place He becomes "a little sanctuary" to us. He draws us with the cords of His love. He embraces our soul, warms it with His love and seals His word upon our heart. We get glimpses of His glory, so that all doubt as to who is beside us is taken away. "Surely the Lord is in this place." We knew a man who, night after night, and under the light of the stars, enjoyed much communion with Christ. Sometimes, as he kneeled on the heather beside a stone which jutted out of the ground, he watered it with his tears. Years afterwards when he came in view of that spot of sweet and hallowed memories he broke down and wept. Our Bethel hours, on the other hand, may be in the public means of grace. We remember an evening long ago walking out of a meeting house behind an elderly woman. When someone apologised to her for the length of the service she said: "Oh, I could have stayed there for ever." The Lord gave her a drink from the river of His pleasure. Such hours are precious beyond words. We remember them with a touch of holy nostalgia, and sometimes long for the day when our Bethel shall never come to an end. It is good to know that the God who is in Heaven is also down in this lower vale in daily communion with His people. "Whom have I in heaven but Thee; and there is none upon earth that I desire beside Thee." He is here as well as there. "The God of Bethel" is also :

V. A God to be confessed. It may be that you are here who, in the secret place, have often poured out your soul before the Lord, yet you have never confessed Him as your God before man. The Lord values our secret exercises and confessions, but let me remind you that He has also commanded us to confess Him before men. Let us not be ashamed to own Him as our Lord. Whatever timidity and fears may lodge in our hearts we should never conceal the worth of our inheritance or whose we are and whom we serve. He is not ashamed to call **us** brethren. He confessed us before men. "These", He said, "are my mother, my sister and my brother." The voice in which God expresses His love to His people reverberates, as it were, throughout all creation. "And I heard a great voice out of Heaven saying, Behold, the tabernacle of God is with men, and He will dwell with them, and they shall be His people, and God himself shall be with them and be their God." Both your past sins and your present infirmities may discourage you from paying your vows before the Lord in His people's company and in the presence of the world. But remember His promise: "My grace is sufficient for thee, for my strength is made perfect in weakness." Mary confessed Him in the presence of Judas and before His apostles. "She hath done what she could . . . and wheresoever this Gospel shall be preached throughout the whole world this also that she hath done shall be spoken of for a memorial of her." To confess the Lord is one of our greatest privileges here. The Church, in The Song, though confessing herself to be "black", would, on the other hand, describe Him to Jerusalem's daughters and say: "This is my Beloved, and this is my friend, O ye daughters of Jerusalem."

Let me end our brief meditation by saying that however sweet and precious our Bethel hours may be here, we must not tarry on this mount. This is not our rest. The Lord's people are strangers and pilgrims in this world — seeking that city which hath foundations. They shall all at last be gathered to Shiloh, their glorious Redeemer. There, their sun shall no more go down. Till then let us, like Jacob, wait for His salvation till the day break and the shadows flee away.

Are there those in my hearing to whom the God of Bethel is a stranger? Do not despise Him who is speaking to you from Heaven. Make Christ your own, and then you shall be of those who say, "The Lord is the portion of my soul." "For God is the portion of Jacob." Without Him, whatever else we may have, we shall remain in a state of eternal misery. Why not make Him your own this day? Happy are the people whose God is the Lord. Amen.

III

GILEAD'S BALM

"Is there no balm in Gilead; is there no physician there? Why then is not the health of the daughter of my people recovered?" (Jer. 8 : 22).

Although these words were primarily addressed to Israel when they were in a state of spiritual decline, they must be given a much wider application than what they have in their original context. Since the gospel, the good news of God's Salvation, is by Christ's command to be preached to all men, and since all men are in the fatal grip of sin, this solemn question is, therefore, addressed to all. And although the question is addressed to all who come within the joyful sound of the gospel it is, on the other hand, personal to each one of us. In our relationship with God we stand accountable and alone, as if no creature existed within the universe but ourselves. Each of us shall at last have to stand before God to give an account of our deeds in this life whether they be good or evil. And the greatest sin which we can commit in this life is to neglect the great salvation and to ignore the Great Physician who alone can heal our souls. Let us look, briefly, at these words. We notice, first:

I. The Disease of Sin

Let us hear, first of all, what God Himself has to say about this disease. When we are stricken with sickness, it is not for us to say what the nature of our trouble is. It is for the physician to diagnose our sickness and, if that is possible, to prescribe a cure. Men may have their own views of sin, but if these deny or contradict what God says about it in His Word, they are to be rejected as false and spurious and of no importance at all. He who is our Creator is the One who knows all things. He has made a diagnosis of this disease, and if we are wise it is to His voice we listen. This subject, however, is so vast, so deep and terrible that we can only mention a few aspects of it.

The first thing that God says about this disease is that it is a **universal condition.** "All have sinned." "There is none righteous, no not one." Adam was the federal head of mankind, so that when he fell away from God we all fell and sinned in him and

with him. And the loathsome disease which took possession of
his nature extends to all men. None of those who enter this world
by ordinary generation has escaped this deadly plague. Its destructive power works in the hearts and lives of all men.

It is a disease which is also **co-extensive with the whole of our
being.** There are those who say that although man has fallen a
prey to sin he is still capable of doing good, and that there is still
much in his nature which God accepts and recognises as good.
While by human categories we classify men as "good" and 'bad",
God, who knows the heart, pronounces us all without soundness
or health. Before His eyes the heart of man is "desperately wicked"
and, in the depth of its depravity, it is only known to Him. And
when God speaks of the "heart" He means the whole of our
nature and the whole bent and bias of our minds, our wills and of
all our inward desires. We were "born in sin and shapen in
iniquity", and to our original sin we add actual transgressions
which greatly aggravate our state and plight. The world in which
we live is, for example, a pale reflection of the heart of man.
From whence come the wars, the confusions, the lawlessness, the
indescribable abominations which threaten our destruction in
these days? They have their source in the human heart, and if
the present process of degeneration continues one wonders how
long can the Lord bear with us. The contaminating plague which
— as in other days — is in danger of destroying our world has
its source in man's sinful nature. And those to whom God has
given a true insight into their own heart can only bow their heads
in shame and helplessness and say, "God be merciful to me, a
sinner." They say with another: "In me, that is in my flesh,
dwelleth no good thing."

"For a disease that loathsome is
So fills my loins with pain."

There was a law in Israel which demanded that the leper should
be excluded from society, and from all access to God's house.
Wherever this contagion was discovered he immediately became
an outcast, till such a time as he found healing. And the greatest
loss that man has suffered from sin is that **it has broken off his
communion with God.** If, then, we are not delivered from this
disease we shall be eternally separated from God and excluded
from the bliss of Heaven. The moment this evil thing touched
the beings of those angels "who kept not their first estate" they
were banished into the outer darkness. The moment the devil's
breath touched the soul of man, and man, "left to the freedom of
his own will", yielded to Satan's lie, he lost communion with God
and was banished from paradise. On the great day which awaits

us all the Judge on the Throne shall banish from His presence
all who are undelivered from this plague. "Depart from me." To
use an illustration, if a person came to your door whom you
knew to be carrying a deadly contagion you would not say to
him: "Come in. You are welcome here. Sit down with my children.
My home is yours." No, you would wisely shun such a person
and exclude such a danger from your home. And into God's
Home above nothing shall enter that "defileth or worketh
abomination or maketh a lie." The imperatives of Heaven cannot
be by-passed. We must be renewed or healed in the inner man;
washed in the blood of the Lamb, clothed in Emmanuel's
righteousness, and made sweet and pure through the sanctification
of the Holy Spirit. Heaven is not for the ungodly or for those
who remain in the grip of this plague.

And for this disease there is no cure on earth. In the days of
the prophet there were false preachers who minimised the evil
of sin and who healed the wound of the daughter of Zion lightly,
saying: "Peace, peace." And are we not familiar in these times
with those who put soft deceptive pillows under the head of
perishing sinners. Instead of exposing the evil of sin, they cover
it up by making vague statements that all is well. There are also
on the scene those who speak of sin as something the source of
which is in our external environment or in the example of our
fellow men. But such superficial explanations are far removed
from reality. All the evils which surface today before our eyes
have, as we have said, their source in the human heart, and till
the heart is changed by the Holy Spirit there is no hope for man.

This is a disease therefore which, without the help and power
of God, **must end in total and eternal death.** "For the wages of
sin is death." God warned man as to the consequence of sin.
"In the day that thou eatest thereof thou shalt surely die." This
was not the threat of mere physical death. When man sinned,
and God withdrew His presence from his soul, his soul pined
away in utter death. "The soul that sinneth it shall die." And
eternal death follows in the wake of spiritual death.

Not very long ago I met a man who was led to seek the Lord
through the words which a minister used in one of his public
prayers. "Lord," he said, "there are millions with Thee in glory
who were born in sin and who lived in sin; but not one who died
in sin." The words arrested this man's mind and brought him
under spiritual concern which resulted in his conversion. O! that
these words would arrest us all and lead us to seek the great
salvation which Christ alone can give.

Perhaps the most terrible thing one could say about this disease is that it may be working within our beings without our having any awareness of it. The soul, while dead in trespass and sin, may lie on the lap of a fond delusion that all is well when all is ill. There are instances in the Bible of men and people who were moving toward eternal death while, at the same time, they thought their lives and works were perfect before God. The Pharisee who stood before God in the temple to pray had no awareness of his spiritual sickness. The Church at Laodicea looked upon herself as whole — with no need of the Physician. Sin is a drug. In the coma or dream of spiritual death, we think favourably of ourselves. In this state we think we are whole and that we therefore need not a physician. The man or woman who has no awareness of the plague of his or her own heart is, indeed, in a state of great danger. There is hope for those who know themselves to be sick, for they may be led to seek healing through Christ and His balm. Our prayer should be that God would awaken us out of the sleep of death lest we find ourselves at last in the dread place where sleep is unknown, and where sin shall rage for ever and ever within our beings.

But for all who believe what God says in His Word of our state by nature, and who have, in some measure, felt the plague of their own heart, there is:

II. A Physician and a Balm

The Physician of the soul is God Himself. "I am the Lord that healeth thee." He who created us in His own image, and who knows perfectly the nature and extent of our "hurt" is our Healer. He alone could provide "a balm", the healing virtues of which can never fail: "Who healeth all thy diseases". Whatever destructive inroads sin has made in our hearts and lives God can still restore us to full spiritual health. If, in the words of another, all the people of God are in this life in His hospital none ever dies there — or ever shall. They are all in His hand, each and all blessed with His loving and personal care. "The Lord will strengthen him upon the bed of languishing: "Thou wilt make all his bed in his sickness."

O! how we ought to admire and wonder at the condescension of God in all this. Are we not amazed that He who counts the numbers of the stars, and who gives them all their names, the Creator and the Sustainer of the great universe in which we live, should, in unspeakable love and tenderness, bind up all the wounds of His ailing people. He is ever beside all who are broken in their hearts and whose cry is, "Heal my soul, for I have sinned against thee." The pity of an earthly father toward his child is but a pale illustration of the pity which flows from the very heart of God towards poor ailing sinners who seek salvation at His hand.

It was this that constrained Him to enter our world in our nature. "He came to bind up the broken hearted." He took "bone of our bone and flesh of our flesh". He took our sins and our sorrows, and although He is now exalted at God's right Hand He is still the true Physician of souls.

The Gospels are full of instances of His mercy, power, and grace as these were exercised in the salvation of those who had no help of man, and who in looking to their left hand and their right saw none who could save them. The bowed-down and broken woman who had spent her all on other physicians found, when in an act of faith she touched the hem of His garment, her terrible disease removed. She was made whole. Healing power had flowed from the Great Physician which consciously surged through her whole being. She was but one of many. She was but one of the great multitude which no man can number whom Christ shall present to Himself "without spot or wrinkle or any such thing". His healing is perfect healing. It is not something which gives temporary relief only to return again. No. It is radical. It is permanent. It is not the old creature patched up for a while. The man whom God heals is for ever a new creature in Christ. He is renewed in all his faculties and, in the moment of his regeneration, put in possession of eternal health. The Spirit of God, who is the author of regeneration, shall, by a work of sanctification, bring all the people of God to perfection. "They shall stand without fault before the Throne."

But how and where does the sinner particularly find healing? What is the balm which the Lord applies to his wounds? There are many opinions as to what, literally and exactly, the balm of Gilead was. In the opinion of many who have studied the historical setting of this verse "the balm of Gilead" was the substance of a tree which grew in this region. The healing balsam flowed out of the tree after it was cut, and had virtues peculiar to itself. There were also physicians in Gilead skilled in the application of this balm. We know that these words are proverbial. They are also typical of the healing power of Christ both in His death and life.

There is no healing or salvation for the soul of man apart from the death of Christ. He is "the Tree of Life" who was, at the same time, "wounded for our transgressions and bruised for our iniquities." "By His stripes we are healed." Before healing or life could come to man, Christ must endure the stroke of Divine Justice. When man sinned that sword stood between him and the tree of life, but now we are reconciled to God by the death of His Son. It is in beholding the Lamb of God — Christ crucified — that the soul is saved and that we are given access to all the blessings of redemption. Those who were dying in the camp of Israel, through the sting of the fiery serpents which raged among them, found instant healing in looking to the serpent on the pole. "As Moses lifted up the serpent in the wilderness even so must the Son of Man be lifted up that whosoever believeth in Him should not perish, but have everlasting life." Where do you, dear friend, find healing for a wounded spirit and a guilty conscience? How did you enter into peace with God? Where did the oppressive burden of sin fall from your soul? Where, but at the Cross of Calvary and through the blood of sprinkling. His death is our balm. It is from the wounds of Christ, who is the Tree of Life, that the balsam of salvation flows.

It is through His death also that free and saving grace is bestowed on us. "By grace we are saved." And the grace which saves is the grace which heals the soul. When Satan threw his darts into the soul of Paul, His great Physician in Heaven applied His balm to his wounded spirit. "My grace is sufficient for thee, for my strength is made perfect in weakness." You recall how on the day of Atonement in Israel, when the high priest sprinkled the blood of the Covenant before the mercy seat, God's glory which dwelt between the Cherubims did, in the words of the Psalm, shine forth. And when the sinner is reconciled to God through the death of His Son not only does grace reign in his heart but the first rays of the Sun of Righteousness shine into his soul. Christ, the Eternal Sun, rises on his soul with healing in His wings.

God's Word also brings healing to the afflicted soul. "He sent His Word and healed them." It was by His Word that He healed many while He was among us. He said to the Leper, "I will, be thou clean. And immediately his leprosy departed from him." This is the universal testimony of true Christian experience. You may recall the day, when pining in the very shades of death, He passed by you and spoke a word to your soul. How dear and precious to your heart is that word which first brought healing and comfort to your spirit. It was as if God's life-giving lips had touched your soul. "Say unto my soul, I am Thy salvation." "The leaves of the tree are for the healing of the nations." It is through the application of His promises by the Holy Spirit that the Lord heals and purifies the soul. "Sanctify them through the truth: Thy Word is truth". But not till we reach that happy country "where the inhabitant shall not say, I am sick", shall all our hurts be fully recovered. Meantime, let us who know His name, continue instant in prayer that His balm may bring more and more comfort to our broken and contrite spirit till the day dawn and the day-star arise in our hearts.

It were well for us to observe where this balm is. Literally speaking, Gilead was not remote from the daughter of Zion or the people of Israel. It was within easy reach of all who sought a cure for their hurt. And spiritually the same is true. "The Word is nigh thee, even in thy mouth and in thine heart; that is, the word of faith which we preach." We have the Word of God in our homes, and often in our hands. Parts of it we have even stored in our memory. But is it in our heart? Do we believe it? Do we receive Him who is present in His Word? Gilead, or the means of grace, is near — and yet, for those who do not believe, so far. Is not the same true of the Throne of Grace? "Draw nigh unto God, and He will draw nigh unto you." He is **waiting** to be gracious. You may kneel before God in the privacy of your own little room in your home and ask Him to save you. You may do it inwardly, even where you are at this moment, sitting and listening to the Word. You are without excuse. "The word is nigh thee." O! the deep and solemn tragedy of entering a lost eternity because we refuse to believe — because we refuse to come to Christ. Why should you be so unjust and unkind to your own soul as, by your neglect, to involve it in eternal deprivation, destruction and despair? That is what you are doing who do not avail yourselves of God's loving kindness. Just think of the consequences of your neglect in all their terror; but, is it not true that they cannot really bear thinking about.

Then there is:

III. **The Great and Solemn Question:** "Why then is the health of the daughter of my people not recovered?"

If this plague is so deadly, and if both the Physician and the balm are accessible and available, why then are we not healed? At the bar of this question each sinner may have his or her own excuse. One may say— "I have no awareness of this disease. I have no conviction that my state is such as you describe. Till this is given me I cannot do anything." But, as we have tried to show, it is not what you feel about it, but what God says about it, and what He wants you to do, that matters. One may be dying of a malignant disease without having any pain; but the absence of pain is no proof that all is well or that the disease is not doing its destructive work. Whatever our "feelings" may be, we are all, without Christ, in the grip of death.

There are others who may be in the hands of false physicians.

We live, spiritually speaking, in the age of quacks and cults. All and each of these have their own spurious prescriptions and cures. Think, for example, of the millions who put themselves in the hands of a priest believing that he has the power to put away their sins, and to pave a way for them to Heaven. But, there is but one name under Heaven given among men whereby we must be saved, even the name of Jesus. Pass **Him** by and you sink into woe.

Others there are who play fast and loose with time and privilege. Satan may agree with them that they need salvation, but he whispers, as in the case of the Rich Fool, that there are still "many years" and a bright long future awaiting them. There is always, he tells them, tomorrow, or the "more convenient time". Alas, a lost eternity is a place of regrets. We carry our memory with us to the world of spirits. "Son, remember", were the words which Abraham addressed to the rich man in torments. He had no thought of death when death came. Dear friend, redeem your time; and while Jesus of Nazareth is passing by in the loving overtures of the Gospel, lift up your voice and cry for salvation. Wilt **thou** be made whole? May Christ, the Physician, be precious to us all, and may the Balm of His grace, applied by the Holy Spirit to our souls, mark the beginnings of our everlasting joy.

IV

" WE SHALL BE LIKE HIM "

"Beloved, now are we the sons of God, and it doth not yet appear what we shall be; but we know that when He shall appear we shall be like Him, for we shall see Him as He is. And every man that hath this hope in him, purifieth himself even as He is pure." (John III : v. 2, 3).

Without waiting to give these words an extended introduction we may go on to consider:

I. **The Present Privilege of God's People:** "How are we the sons of God . . . "

Literally there are two ways in which we may enjoy membership in a family. The one is by birth and the other is by adoption. By human law it is, of course, unnecessary to be adopted into the family into which we are born. Our birth into the family entitles us to the privileges which belong to it. But within the family of God both are necessary. God in His Word declares that without a new spiritual birth we can have no place within this family. This is one of the great requirements of Heaven. Nicodemus, for example, was a religious man. He followed the pattern of a formal, traditional religion. He was, by modern standards, a college professor. His outward life was morally correct. In his own eyes he was already within God's Kingdom. He was by birth an Israelite, and therefore a member of God's Church. When, however, he stood before Christ, and when he asked Him a question with regard to His power and miracles, our Lord simply said, "Verily, verily, I say unto thee, ye must be born again." This was not an irrelevant answer to his question. Our Lord knew that the natural man, however learned or however religious, can never receive or understand the things of God. They are indeed, foolishness to him. Without, for example, being born into the world of nature we would know nothing of that world. We would, in fact, have no real existence at all. The same, and in a deeper sense, is true spiritually. There can be no apprehension or understanding of the spiritual world — which belongs to another dimension entirely — unless we are born into it. "How can these things be?" was the question which exposed Nicodemus for what he was in a state of spiritual death or blindness. He was ignorant of the very beginnings of the true Christian life, and of the experience which God's people value because it marks their entrance into God's kingdom and into communion with, and knowledge of, the only living and true God. Men are by nature dead in their trespass and in their sin, and as such they cannot know or have any fellowship with Him Who is "the God of the living."

We heard once of two men who met each other in the way. They had never seen one another before. "What," said the one to the other, "is that which never was, which never is, and which never shall be?" The answer was— "That which never was, which never is, and which never shall be is that a child not reborn should be in my Father's house." The question and the answer were spiritual, for they were both spiritual men.

The Church in heaven in known as "the Church of the first-born." The names of God's elect were in the Lamb's Book of Life before the world was, but just as our names are registered by law in the books of the nation when we are naturally born, God also has our names written in that heavenly Book in which is recorded our entrance into His Kingdom. The Book of Life is the Book of the Living.

"And it of Zion shall be said
This man and that man there
Was born: and he that is Most High
Himself shall stablish her.

When God the people writes
He'll count that this man born was there . . . "

In the realm of grace our rebirth and adoption go together. Both, as we said, are necessary. Although the people of God were chosen and loved in Christ from all eternity they were, in their fallen state, "strangers and foreigners to God". They were the children of wrath even as others. They were darkness, in a kingdom of darkness and under the sway and dominion of the prince of darkness. In a state of sin they were the children of the wicked one. But God translated them and adopted them out of that state into His own Kingdom and family. This was an act of sovereign grace the wonder beyond all knowledge.

In these acts of grace there is a manifestation both of God's power and of God's love. In the epistle to the Ephesians Paul ascribes the spiritual resurrection or conversion of believers to "the exceeding greatness" of God's power. They were held by a power which they could never break or overcome. Sin, Satan and Death held them in their grasp. Only God Himself could open their prison door, break the chains which bound them, and give them to know the glorious liberty of the children of God. "Thy people shall be willing in the day of Thy power." The new birth then is a display of the effectual working of the Holy Spirit in bringing the soul from death to life. But there is also a revelation of God's love. "Behold, what manner of love the Father hath bestowed upon us that we should be called the sons of God." How wonderful to all the people of God is this love. David in speaking of Jonathan's love to him placed it in this category. "Thy love to me was wonderful." But that love was but a small reflection of Christ's love to His People in making them all, by this act of adoption, His sons and daughters. If Paul prayed that his Ephesian converts might know the exceeding greatness of God's power in their conversion he also prayed that they might, with all the saints, be able to comprehend that love which passeth knowledge. It was this love which made them fellow citizens with the saints and members of the household of God.

We knew a man who, after he had tasted that the Lord is gracious, was so filled with amazement that God should love and embrace such a vile creature as he was, and that He would give to such an one a right to all the privileges and blessings of His redeemed people, felt that when he entered heaven he would "for a thousand years" bow his head at the wonder that such an one should be there. And this truly is a wonder that shall ever lodge in the breast of all His people.

The evidence of this change, both of our nature and of our relationship to God, is two-fold. The one is inward and the other is outward. "He that believeth on the Son of God hath the witness in himself." In the new born soul there is a love for holiness and an aversion to sin. Sin is what gives grief to the believer. The good that he would do he cannot do because evil is present with him. This conflict between grace and sin, or between the law of God inscribed by the Holy Spirit on the renewed soul, and the law of of sin remains while we are in this tabernacle.

There is also a love to Christ and to all His people. They say that when a child is born into the natural world he brings with him into that world a natural, or instinctive, love for his parents and also for those who make up the family. Be that as it may, we know that love to God and to all His people is in every renewed heart. "We know that we have passed from death unto life because we love the brethren." It begins with Christ, "the Elder Brother" in heaven, and extends to all the mystical body both in heaven and on earth. The true believer embraces in his or in her affections all the people of God. They say with Ruth— "Thy people shall be my people and thy God, my God."

And as new born babes they desire the sincere milk of the Word. This is another evidence of their being His. Their mouth is open to receive God's Word. By faith they receive of the fulness which is in Christ. They are a people who hunger and thirst after righteousness and who therefore have the promise that God shall supply all their needs according to His riches in glory by Christ Jesus. By the spirit of adoption they cry "Abba, Father" and say, "Give us this day our daily bread". And in His house there is bread enough and to spare. His table is furnished with good things, which all His children are invited to enjoy.

Do they not also prove themselves to be God's children by receiving and enduring the Lord's chastisement when that is needed? "Whom the Lord loveth He chasteneth and scourgeth every son whom he receiveth." "As many as I love I rebuke and chasten." It is in his chastisements that we often see His love, His faithfulness and wisdom. In these also we often discover our own follies. "Before I was afflicted I went astray."

But there is **the outward evidence** of their sonship as well. As the child may bring a natural love for his family into the world, family likeness may also be imprinted on his very face. This is often, as we know, a fact of nature. And the new creature in Christ bears the image of the heavenly. "We all, with open face, beholding as in a glass the glory of the Lord, are changed into the same image from glory to glory even as by the Spirit of the Lord." They are epistles of Christ that may be known and read of all men. The question was asked of old, "Who is she that looketh forth as the morning, clear as the sun, fair as the moon and terrible as an army with banners?" Who but the children of the day of whom Christ said, "Ye are the light of the world." Their light is derived or borrowed from the Sun of Righteousness. God's people answer to the description which the Lord gives of them in His Word. They abstain from all appearance of evil while, at the same time, they are in the footsteps of the flock. The Lord's people see but little of His likeness in themselves. Mercy and Christiana, in the "Pilgrim's Progress", could not discern in themselves what the one could see in the other. We say, "my spot is not the spot of thy children." Ruth said to Boaz that she was not, either in grace or beauty, like his handmaids, but he saw a loveliness in her which she could not see in herself. It is good to reflect in our life and conversation the unconscious image of Him who hath begotten us unto a lively hope. Moses wist not that his face shone. It was he who prayed: "And let the beauty of the Lord our God be upon us."

Now notice, in the second place:

II. Their Future Hope

"We know not what we shall be, but we know that when He shall appear we shall be like Him for we shall see Him as He is." In the words of Thomas Manton there is a mist on eternity. The future state of the redeemed within the veil, and the kingdom which they are to inherit, they can only see through a glass darkly. It is God's glory to hide a thing. We know something of what we were, where we were and how we were. We know our present infirmities, our crosses and burdens, our fears and conflicts. We mourn over our leanness and the years which the locusts have eaten. Our sins are ever before us. **But we know not what we shall be.**

Needless to say our relationship with Christ through our regeneration and justification is the same now as it shall be in heaven; but with regard to the glory that shall be revealed in God's redeemed, we know only in part. Who can envisage a world, or a state of existence, without sin, without sorrow, without temptation or without weakness of mind or body? Heaven is the place where the inhabitant shall not say "I am sick". Christ shall present His people to Himself without spot or wrinkle or any such thing. When John gazed upon the great multitude which no man could number he knew not who they were. Their glory, happiness and songs made them a great wonder even in Heaven. Surely that great multitude did not belong to this fallen world. But they did. In that multitude there were some whom he knew on earth, and who had passed through great tribulation, but they were now, in the light of God's face, shining as the brightness of the firmament and as the stars for ever and ever. How inconceivable is the change that shall take place in our translation from grace on earth to glory in Heaven!

> Though ye have lien among the pots
> Like doves ye shall appear
> Whose wings with silver, and with gold
> Whose feathers covered are.

And we know not what we shall have. In this life we have but the earnest of good things to come. The Lord, indeed, gives His people here a foretaste of all the blessings which they are to enjoy in Heaven. The supreme joy of Heaven has its source in the full and everlasting enjoyment of God. In this life their fellowship is with the Father and with His Son, Jesus Christ. The love of

Christ is also shed abroad in their hearts. But here these enjoyments come and go. Their brook often dries. Seasons there are when they mourn over the absence of the Beloved and when their hearts feel empty and cold. Although they are heirs of God and joint-heirs with Jesus Christ, they speak of themselves as poor and needy. But when they shall come of age they shall possess the unsearchable riches of Christ reserved in Heaven for them. This is all their desire, and there is no desire implanted by the Spirit of God in their hearts but God shall satisfy. In that day "they shall hunger no more, neither thirst any more, for the Lamb who is in the midst of the Throne shall feed them, and shall lead them to living fountains of waters, and God shall wipe away all tears from their eyes." The sweet "crumbs" which now fall from His hand and which sustain them on their wilderness journey, only increase their longings for the fullness prepared for them above.

We could also say that **we know not where we shall be.** Heaven is the eternal home of the redeemed. They are born from above and for that reason God has created a longing in their souls for that city which they are seeking. Heaven in the highest sense of the word is God Himself. "Lord, thou hast been our dwelling place in all generations." Not only has He been their home in this world of time, but "from everlasting to everlasting". They had a place in His heart and in His purpose of grace from all eternity. Their life is now hid with Christ in God. At Bethel, Jacob said— "The Lord is in this place . . . this is none other than the house of God and this is the gate of Heaven."

But Heaven is also a place. It is the city of the Great King. "I go," said our Lord, "to prepare a **place** for you." It is the land wherein dwelleth righteousness. There are moments in the life of God's people when they get a glimpse not only of the King in His beauty, but also of this land of far distances. Moses saw the good land from the top of Pisgah. We also see it by faith. We look at the things which are unseen and eternal. And what they see by faith detaches them from things seen. They have the heart and walk of pilgrims and strangers on the earth. They are on the way Home. But how little we know of that glorious abode! Not till we cross the river shall we know the glory and the bliss of that Kingdom which is "incorruptible and undefiled, and that fadeth not away." It is not sweet to think that although we are still in the world of time, each one of His people may enjoy a little heaven here under His wings. Under His wings we have protection, we have nearness to Him, we have warmth and fellowship, we have unspeakable joy.

"In shadow of thy wings I'll joy
For thou my help hast been."

Although, dear friends, we know not yet what we shall be, **"we know that when He shall appear we shall be like Him for we shall see Him as He is."** This is the great hope of the people of God — that they shall see His face in righteousness. "I shall be satisfied when I awake with Thy likeness." Before He left this world He gladdened the hearts of His people by giving them all a great promise. "And ye now therefore have sorrow; but I will see you again, and your heart shall rejoice, and your joy no man taketh from you." When Job was in great depths of sorrow this was the one bright star in his sky. "Whom I shall see for myself and not another." And they shall see Him as **He is.** Not as He was. John and many of his contemporaries saw Him in a state of humiliation and grief. They saw Him in the likeness of sinful flesh. They saw Him bearing a crown of thorns. They saw Him rejected and despised of men, and a homeless Wanderer in this cold world. But there **we shall see Him as He is** in all His exalted glory. We shall see Him at God's Right Hand "crowned with many crowns". In that happy world their sun shall no more go down. No cloud shall ever come between them and Christ, the bright and morning Star.

Let me say this one word. Would you go to a Christless heaven? If you would you will never be in heaven. If the Church, who is Christ's bride, were to get the mansions and riches of the heavenly world, and Christ absent, do you think she would be happy? No! Her cry would be, "Saw ye Him whom my soul loveth?" This, needless to say, cannot happen. We simply want to stress again the truth that all the well-springs of the people of God are in Christ. Their love rests on Him "Whom having not seen ye love; in whom though now ye see Him not, yet believing, ye rejoice with joy unspeakable and full of glory." We rejoice in the hope of seeing Him as He is.

Now the fulfilment of this promise is not something remote or far away. "When He shall appear." He is to appear to each of His people when they leave this scene of time. Then their souls immediately pass into glory. Absent from the body they are present with the Lord. He shall appear on the last day when their bodies shall also be redeemed, and when all His people shall be gathered to Him. Meantime let us watch, pray and wait, till the day break and the shadows flee away. "My soul waiteth for the Lord more than they who watch for the morning."

Finally notice :

III. The Constant Exercise of God's People

"And every man that hath this hope in him purifieth himself even as he is pure." Heaven is a place of infinite purity. Nothing shall enter there "that defileth or which maketh a lie." God's people know that without holiness no man shall see the Lord. They are therefore at the Throne of grace asking the Lord to wash them with hyssop and to create in them a clean heart. "Having, therefore, these promises dearly beloved, let us cleanse ourselves from all filthiness of the flesh and spirit, perfecting holiness in the fear of God." The Church here is like a bride who is preparing herself to enter into Her Lord's presence in the mansions above. "The marriage of the Lamb is come, and His wife hath made herself ready." This is their desire — to be like Him. Long ago I sat down in a church and listened to a faithful minister of Christ as he spoke about the longing after true and perfect holiness which is in the heart of God's people. "This is a people," he said, "who would make their bed in hell rather than entertain the hope that they could enter heaven with one sin in their soul." He who has His fire in Zion and His furnace in Jerusalem shall refine His people as gold till His own image is perfectly reflected in each one of them. In the heavenly world they shall all be like little mirrors in which Christ may see His own image perfectly reflected. The blood of sprinkling is also ever available. "They washed their robes and made them white in the blood of the Lamb."

My dear fellow sinners who are still in darkness, "without God and without hope in the world", there is also an eternity of woe of which you know but little. As there is a wise concealment on the part of God with regard to the glorious destiny awaiting His people, what our Lord says of the terrors of a lost eternity should alarm us and stir us into a state of spiritual concern. Those who are in hell knew but little on earth of what hell is like. May none of us here, who are still in the room of mercy, enter into those dungeons of everlasting despair. Listen to what He says— "For God so loved the world that He gave His only begotten Son that whosoever believeth in Him should not perish but have ever-lasting life." If you come to Christ, and embrace Him as your own, then you also shall have a good hope through grace and shall know the good of His chosen people. And if you come let me assure you that a welcome awaits you, for "This Man receiveth sinners."

V

" THE JOYFUL SOUND "

"Blessed is the people that know the joyful sound: they shall walk, O Lord, in the light of Thy countenance." (Ps. 89 : 15).

In this inconceivably precious Psalm, there are great truths, great promises and prophecies, which cannot but bring joy to the hearts of God's people. In it we read of God's everlasting covenant with the Church in Christ who is her Head; of His power to save and keep all who trust in Him; of His faithfulness and love towards all the heirs of salvation, and of the way in which His infinite perfections come to light in the work of redemption. The revelation, or declaration, of these truths, and of many more besides, is truly a "joyful sound" to His own people. Let me this evening offer a few comments on these words. Let us think first of:

I. The Joyful Sound and what it is

To an Israelite the "joyful sound" might have meant some of those events which stood related to the Old Dispensation. There are, to begin with, those who associate the words with the great Day of Atonement. On that day the High Priest divested himself of the garments of beauty and glory — in which he was habitually clothed in the holy place — and put on the holy linen robe in which he was to minister in the most holy place. In the one hand he carried the blood of the Covenant, and in the other the golden vessel of incense. With these offerings he entered "within the veil" where he sprinkled the blood before the Mercy Seat on which, between the Cherubims, the divine glory permanently rested. Sin was typically put away. Atonement was made. And when the high priest re-appeared before the people the trumpets gave forth their joyful sound, and the people came forward with their sacrifices of praise. God had embraced them anew. Peace, through recon- ciliation, was once more established between Him and "the great congregation". Truly this was a day of joy.

These words may be also related to the daily ministry in the holy place where sacrifices were continually offered for the sins of the people. An Israelite, for example, would move toward the outer court of the tabernacle with the lamb which the priest was to offer for his transgressions. There he would place his hand on the head of the lamb and transfer, typically, his guilt to the innocent creature which was presently to die for him. And as the high priest offered to God this sacrifice, and moved within the holy place, the sound of the golden bells which were attached to his robe might be heard in the outer court. The sound of these would declare that atonement was being made for him, that his guilt was put away, and that God had accepted his offering.

A greater occasion than these was the year of Jubilee which was observed in the nation every fifty years. It began with the Day of Atonement. On that glad and longed-for day the trumpets sounded throughout the land to proclaim that all prisoners were released, that all debts were cancelled, that all inheritances forfeited through death or poverty were to be restored, and that all the weary were to rest from toil. It is easy to imagine the joy that would touch the heart of the prisoner in his cave or cell, the poor man oppressed with poverty and toil, or the heart of the widow whose lost inheritance would now be restored, as the trumpets gave their joyful sound in every corner of the land.

But these and other such events were mere typical occasions which pointed to greater events and blessings and which antici- pated the fulfilment of these promises which, like stars, graced the firmament of the Old Testament Dispensation. These promises, types and prophecies were all related to Christ who is both the centre and substance of revelation. Christ is present in the first and in the last promise given to the Church of God in the Scrip- tures of the Old Testament. The first promise speaks of "the seed of the woman" who was to come in the fulness of time to bruise the head of the serpent. The last speaks of "the sun of righteous- ness" or "the bright and morning star", who was soon to arise with healing in His wings on His waiting people and on a fallen world. He therefore commanded us to "search the Scriptures; for in them ye think ye have eternal life; and these are they which testify of me."

The true spiritual Israelite — while rejoicing in those occasions such as we have mentioned — knew that all these pointed to the coming of the Messiah who was to procure everlasting salvation for His people through His obedience and death. Enlightened by the Holy Spirit, and by faith, he knew that behind and beyond all these types and ceremonies God had provided eternal life and peace for all His people through the coming of the Just One. With His coming these types would for ever fade away. They were but mere shadows of good things to come. Think then of the joy that was in the heart of the Old Testament Church as she waited for the coming of her Lord, and as she could already hear the joyful sound of His voice in His Word! "The voice of my beloved, behold, he cometh, leaping upon the mountains, skipping upon the hills." She could already hear the sound of His footsteps coming over the mountains of time and separation.

The coming of our Redeemer into the world was therefore the occasion of the greatest joy, we believe, ever known in Heaven or on earth. On that night the heavenly host sang above our world. "Glory to God in the highest and on earth peace, and good will toward men." A world "living in the wicked one", and ruined by sin, became the scene of the greatest manifestation of God's love ever given to men or angels. "For God so loved the world that He gave His only begotten Son that whosoever believeth in Him should not perish but have everlasting life." The New Testament is replete with lovely stories of the joy which the coming of Christ brought to His own waiting people. How wonderful, for example, are the words of Elisabeth who, when Mary who bore the Holy Child Jesus in her womb arrived at her door, exclaimed in ecstasy— "For, lo, as soon as the voice of thy salutation sounded in mine ears, the babe leaped in my womb for joy." She had the secret of the Lord with regard to the One who was soon to appear in the world and, in a way too mysterious for words, her joy was communicated to the unborn child who was to be His forerunner on earth.

The question has often been asked as to who were the wise men who, at His birth, came to worship our Lord. To some they were mere superstitious star-gazers. Not so. They, also, had the secret of the Lord in relation to the coming of the Prince of Peace. And there is not in Scripture a lovelier word than that which describes their ecstatic joy when they saw His star, which for the moment had faded from their view. "When they saw the star, they rejoiced with exceeding great joy." That star, with its joyful tidings, brought them to the portals of bliss. Their Redeemer had come. And when they saw Him they fell down and worshipped Him. They did not worship Mary, as the poor benighted papists do. They had no eyes for any creature in Heaven or on earth but for "Jesus only". O! the joy of knowing that Jesus Christ came into the world to save sinners. This is "a joyful sound" that shall deepen and become more wonderful within the breast of every saved man and woman throughout the ages to come. Does it bring joy to us? The same joy was in the heart of Simeon when he took the Holy Child in his arms and blessed God that his eyes had seen His salvation. He was now on the threshold of eternal joy, and he desired to be here no more. "Lord, now lettest thou thy servant depart in peace according to thy word."

The sweetest note in this joyful song is that Christ came to die. He took our nature that in our nature He might die for us. It is no contradiction to say that it is the death of Christ which produces godly sorrow and penitence in our souls, while, at the same time, there is no joy like the joy of knowing that He died to reconcile us to God and to put our sins away "as far as the east is distant from the west". All the blessings of His people come through His death. And these in their number, preciousness and permanence, are unsearchable and beyond number. Take the case of Paul when he penned the words, "The Son of God who loved me and gave himself for me." This was his joyful song on earth. But it was also the source of his sorrow. He remembered his past with its hatred and opposition to the One who loved him. Christ forgave him, but here he could not forgive himself. "They shall look upon Him whom they have pierced and mourn." When Joseph's brethren wept on his shoulder, both sorrow and love filled their hearts. They remembered how they had hated him without cause. Who among God's people ever stood before the Cross of Calvary without grief? It was their sin that nailed their Beloved to the Tree. But the song shall remain, after the years of their mourning have ceased. Heaven is the place of songs. There they sing the song of Moses and of the Lamb. "Unto Him who loved us and washed us from our sins in His own blood . . . to Him be glory and dominion for ever and ever." This is, then, the joyful sound, or song, which has its beginning here, but which shall continue to reverberate through the realms of glory for ever and ever. My friend, do you, through God's grace and forgiveness, know it?

Is it not a joyful sound also to know that He who died rose again from the dead for our justification, and that He ascended up into Heaven where He is making continual intercession for us? By His resurrection "He proved to be the Son of God with power." He overcame death. He robbed the grave of its prey. All those for whom He died shall experience His saving power and participate in His victory. Their spiritual resurrection out of a grave of trespass and sin is the evidence of "the exceeding greatness of His power." This was the song of David.

> "O, Lord, my soul, thou has brought up
> And rescued from the grave."

Was that not a joyful sound which His stricken Bride heard when He passed her by and said, "Live", and when He made her time "a time of love". And their bodies are to share in this great honour and power. "I shall be satisfied, when I awake, with thy likeness."

His ascension and priestly advocacy within the veil are the infallible guarantee that one day we shall see Him as He is and that not one for whom He died shall perish. You recall how He led His disciples out as far as Bethany; and after He had blessed them He was taken up into heaven. Usually when we separate for the last time on earth from our dearest friends we are full of sorrow, but it was not so with those, His followers, when, without His bodily presence and companionship, they moved toward Jerusalem. We are told that "they returned to Jerusalem with great joy, and were continually in the temple praising and blessing God." Why this ecstasy? Just because they knew "the joyful sound": "I am He that liveth and was dead." It was a joy that remained with them amid all their sufferings here. The Lord had gone to prepare a place for them. Because He lived they also would live. They were partakers of the joy with which the hosts of Heaven welcomed the glorious Redeemer and Conqueror as the everlasting doors opened to admit Him, and in Him, all the heirs of salvation into the mansions above. Already they were there in Him. They were there also in their desires, hopes and affections. Their treasure was above.

So you see, dear friends, that both at His entrance into our world and at the hour of His bodily departure into the heavenly kingdom there was a song of joy. Does it end there? Ah, no. Is He not coming again to receive us unto Himself?

In the Epistle to the Hebrews, Paul expounds all that His coming into the world procured for the Church, and he ends his great exposition with the words— "And unto them that look for Him shall He appear the second time without sin unto salvation." He, Himself, gives the promise: "I will come again and receive you unto myself that where I am there ye may be also." His last words to His waiting Bride are: "Behold, I came quickly." And what is her answer? "Even so, come, Lord Jesus."

I shall never forget that summer evening when I entered a Church in the Island of Skye and heard a Psalm being sung by a large congregation.

> "Let heavens be glad before the Lord
> And let the earth rejoice,
> Let seas, and all that is therein
> Cry out and make a noise
> Before the Lord; because He comes;
> To judge the earth come He . . ."   (Ps. 96).

That evening, as in the words of the Psalmist, the inanimate creation was commanded to rejoice at the prospect of His coming, something indescribably sweet and solemn touched my soul. I could, as it were, see through the vistas of future ages the happy day when the Beloved would come to judge the world and to gather His people to Himself. "The joyful sound" which filled my soul that evening was shared, I knew, by the people of God in every age. Again, I ask, is this a joyful sound to you? And we could also give this hope a personal application. While we should acquiesce in the Lord's will for us, and while we would tarry here for a while to do something for Christ "in a day of small things", we look forward to the day when we shall appear in God's presence. How joyful is the sound of His word of promise in this connection. "And they shall see His face and His name shall be in their foreheads."

"They shall be brought with gladness great,
   and mirth on every side,
   Into the palace of the King
   and there they shall abide."

II. The Blessedness of knowing the Joyful Sound

The blessedness, you will notice, consists not in **hearing** the joyful sound but in **knowing** it. To use an example, a stranger might be passing through the land of Israel as the trumpets sounded to proclaim the advent of Jubilee, but their sound might convey little or nothing to him. The joy which touched the hearts of the Israelites at that hour he could not feel, for he was ignorant of the blessings and privileges which the sounds conveyed. And are there not many who sit under the sound of the Gospel who, in their own experience, know nothing of the blessedness of those who are saved, and who, therefore, rejoice in the Lord? To them the Gospel is a savour of death unto death. There are those who have no ear for music; and, similarly, there are many whose inner ear is deaf to "the glad tidings of great joy" which the Gospel proclaims. No man ever spake like the Lord Jesus Christ; yet He condemned many of those who heard His words, but who failed to respond to the glorious overtures of His Gospel. "We have piped unto you and ye have not danced." We may pretend to admire the Gospel, while we fail to respond to the overtures of God's offer of salvation in Christ.

We might say of many of those who know the joyful sound that before it gladdened their heart they heard another voice which filled them with fear and concern. What voice or sound was this? It was God speaking to them from the dark and terrifying precipices of Sinai. God awakened them out of their sleep of death. They came to realise that they were under the just sentence of a broken covenant, and under God's holy and just wrath. They were in the hands of God's Justice, and its hold on them would not, and could not, relax till all its demands were fully satisfied. The thunders of God's law made them fear and tremble exceedingly, for of themselves they had nothing whereby its voice could be silenced. They knew that God was just in the sentence which was pronounced against them.

But the purpose of the Lord in bringing them into such a state of concern, and in making them recognise where they were and how they were, was not their destruction but their salvation. Another voice, therefore, sounded from God's Word. It was the still small voice of peace and acceptance through the merits of Him who died on the Tree. "I, even I, am He that blotteth out thy transgressions for mine own sake, and will not remember thy sins." "As far as the east is from the west, so far hath he removed our transgressions from us." "Who is a God like unto thee, that pardoneth iniquity and passeth by the transgression of the remnant of his heritage? He retaineth not his anger for ever, because He delighteth in mercy." This was the hour when their mourning was turned into dancing, and when an undying love was born in their hearts for Him who died in their room and stead. That was the day when the bells of peace sent their sweet chimes through their conscience and mind. O! friend, was there such an hour in your life? Such an experience marks the beginning of our eternal happiness. As unforgiven sin is the source of everlasting despair, the forgiveness of it is the beginning of our unending joy. And with our forgiveness a new desire to praise the Redeemer is born in our souls.

Heaven is the place where we shall, in perfection, express our indebtedness and happiness to Christ in our praise.

With this love and desire to praise the Lord there is true spiritual discernment. The knowledge which God imparts to His people is seen in the way in which otherwise simple souls, who are but babes in His Kingdom, have a knowledge of the Gospel which is outwith the reach of the wise and the learned of this world. This is one of the evidences that the new creature in Christ is given a knowledge which mere religious formalism or schools of learning can never impart and which belongs to a world they cannot know or enjoy. "That which is born of the flesh is flesh, and that which is born of the Spirit is spirit." "For the natural man receiveth not the things of the Spirit of God; for they are foolishness unto him; neither can he know them, because they are spiritually discerned."

There is no joy in this world to be compared with the joy which the voice of Christ brings to the heart of the gracious soul. "The companions hear thy voice: cause me to hear it." In my younger days I used to hear the Lord's people speak of how Christ would sometimes awake them out of sleep with His Word on their lips. Others would relate how, at the Throne of Grace, God would speak to them out of His written Word of what was relevant to their needs or trials. And others would tell how, unexpectedly, God's Word would become articulate within their spirits, bringing the needed warning or comfort, or anticipating something which was to emerge within the sphere of Providence. Such people knew the Lord and His voice. This was their joy on earth. "Thy statutes have been my songs in the house of my pilgrimage." To the Psalmist God's Word thus given was more precious than gold and sweeter than honey.

III. The Evidence in our life that we know the joyful sound

"They shall walk, O Lord, in the light of thy countenance."

These words mean that they are a people who obey God's voice. To know God savingly is to love and obey Him. Both the mind and the will of God are revealed exclusively in the Written Word. Any word, or tradition of men, which contradicts, adds to, or subtracts from, God's Holy Word is to be rejected, and is rejected by the true believer. An unenlightened world listens to "strangers" whether they be popes, graceless ministers and bishops, or the initiators of ensnaring and deadly religious cults. But God's people listen only to Him.

And the evidence of their obedience is that God is with them in the way. They often say, "Whom have I in Heaven but Thee, and there is none upon earth that I desire beside Thee." This was how God's saints walked in every age. "Enoch walked with God." The Lord speaks of Abraham as His "friend". This is the meaning of those words in the fourth Psalm, "But know that the Lord hath set apart him that is godly for himself." To God's people His presence is often more real than the presence of those who dwell with them in their homes. This is their heaven on earth. "Truly our fellowship is with the Father and with His Son, Jesus Christ."

There are seasons, however, when God's people walk without the light or comfort of His face; but "light is sown for the righteous." "The path of the just is as the shining light, that shineth more and more unto the perfect day." But whether it be in light or shade the Lord will enable us, by His grace, to go "from strength to strength" till we reach the place where we shall see His face without a cloud between.

Dear friend, do you know the joyful sound? Has God ever spoken to your soul: "Son, Thy sins be forgiven thee"? Is the name of Jesus sweet to your ear, since it was He who came to save His people from their sins? If so, one day you will hear His voice welcoming you into that kingdom which fadeth not away. "Come, ye blessed of my Father, inherit the kingdom prepared for you from the foundation of the world." But if we refuse to "kiss the Son", and to give Him our hearts, there is another voice we must listen to. "Depart from me." O! be wise and embrace Christ now. Then, not only would you have joy but we also would rejoice in your salvation. Heaven would rejoice as well. "There is joy in the presence of the angels of God over one sinner that repenteth." Come and welcome to Jesus Christ. Amen.

VI

THE LORD AROUND HIS PEOPLE

" They that trust in the Lord shall be as Mount Zion, which cannot be removed but abideth for ever. As the mountains are around Jerusalem so the Lord is round about His people from henceforth even for ever." (Ps. 125 : 1-2).

Throughout the Bible we often find that the Holy Spirit uses natural figures to illustrate profound spiritual truths and realities. In the words of our text the Church of God, or individual believers, are, in their faith and constancy, compared to Mount Zion, while God Himself in His nearness and protecting power, is compared to the mountains which shelter and surround Jerusalem. Let us look at these words for a moment. Let us consider:

I. The People of God in their Faith and Steadfastness

These are a people who trust in the Lord and who cannot, therefore, be moved. They are a people who trust not in themselves or in any other creature. Their faith does not rest on what they are or on what they do. In this respect they are "a peculiar people", for men in a state of nature are often proud and self-sufficient. They think that by their own imagined goodness they are capable of paving a way into the favour of God. Such men were in the world in the days of our Lord — "men who trusted in themselves that they were righteous." And such men are in the world still. They are men who would place the crown of their salvation on their own head. They would be independent of all help. Although man is in a state of condemnation, without holiness or spiritual ability, he is, left to himself, self-righteous. But "cursed is he that trusteth in an arm of flesh, for he shall be as the heath in the desert which knoweth not when good cometh." And there is no power on earth than can remove this sinful pride and deception within man's heart but the power of God. Only in a day of His power are we made willing to renounce all trust in ourselves and to trust wholly in the Lord for salvation.

Those mentioned in our text are a people who, in relation to their destiny and acceptance with God, have no trust in themselves. There is, of course, so much that we can do in our moral conduct and in our social relationships; but spiritually we are helpless "without God and without hope in the world." There was a day, for example, in the life of Paul when, fixed in his own self-righteousness and deriving all his hope for eternity from his false zeal and from his own correct religious formality, he saw not his need of a Saviour. But Christ brought him into the dust of self-abasement and gave him the sentence of death in his own breast. In that day all trust in himself was for ever slain. He learned that without Christ he had nothing that was pleasing to God, and that he could do nothing to procure his own salvation. From that day he knew that God justified him not by his own works of righteousness but by His sovereign grace and by faith in Christ. He saw that what pleased him was, before God, "as filthy rags", and that weighed in the balances of the sanctuary he infinitely came short of God's glory. Only by faith in the righteousness of Another was he delivered from the bondage and condemnation of sin. From that day Christ alone was the subject of his trust and hope.

This trust in the Lord on the part of His people is all-inclusive. If we are of this number we commit into God's hand not only our persons, but also our times and destiny, and all our cares within the sphere of providence. "Into thine hand I commit my spirit." "Casting all your care upon Him for He careth for you." "My times are in Thy hand." "I have set the Lord always before me." "I know whom I have believed, and am persuaded that He is able to keep that which I have committed unto Him against that day." Such words as these show that they commit themselves wholly and for ever into His hand, "as into the hands of a faithful Creator."

The trust of God's people is pre-eminently in His Word or promise, for the Lord Himself is present in the Word in which they trust. God and His Word are identical. There can be no trust in the one without trust in the other. Those who are His are given "exceeding great and precious promises", and it is of the nature of the true Christian life that God often seals His promises, both in relation to His providence and grace, on their hearts and minds. Although all the promises are the heritage of God's elect, God often makes a personal application of His Word to their souls. And it may often happen that circumstances emerge in their life which seem to nullify His promise. David, in fear and trembling, once asked the question: "Lord, where is Thy former loving kindness which Thou swarest unto David in Thy truth?" "Hath the Lord forgotten to be gracious?" But whatever clouds may overshadow our lives, God's covenant bow of promise is never absent from our sky. How often do we tremble in our nights of trial, but "hitherto hath the Lord helped us." And the God of yesterday is the God of today and of the future. "This God is our God for ever and ever: He will be our guide even unto death." Or, as the words may be translated, "He will be our guide unto death, beyond and over death," and till we reach the place where death is unknown. Such a blessed assurance as this should strengthen our faith and provide us with a song in the night.

Whatever contrary storms, therefore, may break in upon their lives, God's people "cannot be moved". "Their heart is fixed trusting in the Lord." Christ, their Rock and Stay, is the foundation of all their hope. And "the foundation of the Lord standeth sure, having this seal, the Lord knoweth them that are His." Paul, in one place, sits as it were, on the very pinnacle of the universe and surveys all the powers on earth and in hell, which, if they could, would separate the Church from the love of Christ. But how does he end his glorious theme in praise of that love which is stronger than death? "For I am persuaded that neither death nor life, nor angels nor principalities, nor powers, nor things present, nor things to come, nor height, nor depth, nor any other creature shall be able to separate us from the love of God which is in Christ Jesus our Lord." The enemies of the Church never tire of trying to separate her from Christ, but a good hope through grace, which is the anchor of the soul, is both sure and steadfast since it is fixed in Christ the Rock of Ages. Their faith may be small, but in the words of another, "their little faith is in a great God." His love is bound to almighty power and it is by His power they are kept through faith unto salvation. "None perish that trust in Him." "Trust ye in the Lord for ever, for in the Lord Jehovah is everlasting strength." Let us consider also:

II. Their Privilege and Safety

The Lord is about them as the mountains surround Jerusalem. His Israel, in every age, are a people near to Him. They are the subjects of His care. The figure here used is very significant. Let us dwell on it for a moment. What are those mountain ranges, spiritually speaking, which surround the people of God?

He is, to begin with, round about them in His eternal purpose of grace. The Holy Spirit in the Word dwells on this. Where does He begin? "For whom he did foreknow, he also did predestinate . . . and whom he did predestinate them he also called, and whom he called them he also justified and whom he justified them he also glorified." And although these divine acts and decrees have their beginning and their end in the Eternal mind and world, they stand related to the salvation and security of the Church in this world. This purpose has, and shall have, its revelation, fulfilment and consummation, both in the finished work of Christ and in the full redemption of His people. The salvation of the Church, in its origin and consummation, is embraced in that covenant "which is ordered in all things and sure." It was to ratify and procure its promises and provisions that Christ came into the world. The pleasure, or purpose, of the Lord prospered in His hand.

Again, **the infinite merits and righteousness of Christ** stand between the people of God and the perils to which, in a state of sin, they were once exposed. Their sins exposed them to His just wrath, and to the curse of a broken law. But in all His merits as the substitute and surety of His people, He shelters them from those fearful storms which once threatened their destruction. "A man shall be as an hiding place from the wind, and a covert from the tempest, and . . . . as the shadow of a great rock in a weary land," There is no shelter for His Church but in the clefts of the rock. "Our life is hid with Christ in God." It was when the shed blood was sprinkled before the mercy seat that God became a refuge to His people. In was when the blood of the Paschal lamb was sprinkled on their doorposts on the night that the destroying angel was to pass over Egypt, that the safety of Israel was assured. Mount Calvary is pre-eminently the spiritual mountain that gives shelter to the soul. In heaven, "the Lamb in the midst of the throne" shall engage the eyes and affections of all the redeemed for ever and ever; for they know that their eternal happiness and safety have their source in His love in dying for them that He might bring them to God.

This figure also speaks, we believe, of **all the attributes of God which surround His people for ever.** For those who are reconciled to God there is not an attribute in the Godhead but is exercised in their favour. In the words of the Psalm, these are the lofty mountains which bring forth peace unto his people. "We have peace with God, through our Lord Jesus Christ." Through the death of His Son, "mercy and truth are met together, righteousness and peace kiss each other." The righteousness of God which, in the words of another Psalm, is "like the great mountains" is now covered with the golden cloud of God's peace, proclaiming its blessing upon all who kiss the Son. Its frown is changed into a smile. His mercy also encompasses them as a shield. One could

speak of His eternity and His unchangeableness as these stand
related to our everlasting salvation. "I am Jehovah, I change not,
therefore ye sons of Jacob are not consumed." The "I AM" is
He in whose hand are all the saints. "The eternal God is thy
refuge and underneath are the everlasting arms." This is a vast
subject, but those who know the teaching of Scripture know that
the Triune God, in all His perfections, surrounds His own night
and day.

> "I of the Lord my God will say
> He is my refuge still,
> He is my fortress and my God
> And in Him trust I will."

Think also of the **all-availing intercession of our great High
Priest which surrounds His people always.** In heaven He is
making continual intercession for us. The glory and virtue of
His priestly office and acts are derived from Who He is, what
He did, and from the authority which belongs to Him as the
exalted Son of God. God the Father has sealed His office with an
oath. "Thou art a priest for ever after the order of Melchizedek."
This ensures that His prayers are always heard, and that all who
are within the circle of His priestly advocacy shall never perish.
God hears Him always. On earth He prayed, "Father, I will that
they also whom thou hast given me be with me where I am, that
they may behold my glory which thou hast given me, for thou
lovedst me before the foundation of the world." These words shall
continue to rise, like incense before God until the last of His people
arrives in His presence. His intercession is the secret of their preservation. This is what we discover in His words to Peter. "Simon,
Simon, Satan hath desired to have you that he may sift you
as wheat, but I have prayed for thee that thy faith fail not."
That prayer Peter never heard, but he knew from that hour where
his safety lay. It is good to pray for one another, and to have a
place in the prayers of God's people; but the true believer rises
higher than the help of mere man. He trusts in the Lord. "I have
prayed for thee." When a godly woman was once asked by her
friends if they would remember her in their prayers she simply
said: "Prayer is being made for me above." She valued their
prayers but her hope had risen beyond them to the very throne of
God.

Do these words not mean also that **God's Presence is ever with
His people?** Ah, yes. In this way He is around them night and
day . . . "My presence," he said to Moses, "shall go with you and
I will give you rest." "Lo, I am with you alway." We are not to
conclude that the Lord is not with us when we mourn over a

lack of His conscious presence. Our sensible enjoyments of His presence ebb and flow like the tide. But His faithfulness is not dependent on our frames and feelings. We fear sometimes that the Beloved has withdrawn Himself. But what does He say? "Fear not, for I am with thee, I have called thee by thy name. Thou art mine." "I will never" — and this includes every moment of time as well as eternity — "leave thee nor forsake thee." This is what His people have discovered in all the great crises of their life. How real was His presence to Israel as they were passing through the Red Sea! He was a light and shield to them, but a darkness and a terror to their enemies. In the furnace which the king of Babylon prepared to consume the holy children, Christ's presence preserved them from all harm. When the young man who accompanied the prophet trembled as he gazed on their enemies, the prophet of the Lord prayed that his inner eyes might be opened that he might see that He who was with them and for them was mightier and nearer than all their enemies. God and His ministering spirits surrounded the hill. Whatever trials we may have to endure here He will be with us. "Fear not, for I am with thee, be not dismayed, for I am thy God; yea, I will help thee, yea, I will strengthen thee, yea, I will uphold thee with the right hand of my righteousness." How many of the Lord's people in various parts of the world are lonely and for various causes, separated from the public means of grace and from fellowship with their brethren and sisters in Christ. But listen to what He says, "I will be to them as a little sanctuary." He is with each as intimate and personal and loving as He is with all.

The Lord is round them also **in all His great and precious promises.** Many years ago I accompanied a friend in the way. He related to me how the Lord, in answer to prayer, and in the midst of many trials, had upheld him by His word of promise. It was a promise which touched his inward being in the power and comfort of the Holy Spirit. "For this is as the waters of Noah unto me: for as I have sworn that the waters of Noah should no more go over the earth, so have I sworn that I would not be wroth with thee nor rebuke thee. For the mountains shall depart and the hills be removed, but my kindness shall not depart from thee, neither shall the covenant of my peace be removed, saith the Lord that hath mercy on thee." (Is. 54). Since that hour many a sweet drop of comfort have I also derived from these words. Like all the promises of God, it is not only personal to all His people, but it is also confirmed by His oath. Let us therefore keep our eyes fixed on those mountains and say with the Psalmist, "I will lift up mine eyes unto the hills from whence cometh my help. My help cometh from the Lord which made heaven and earth."

Is He not around His people also **in the processes of His Providence?** How solemn and mysterious is this truth! One supreme end of God's providence is to preserve His people. This is what the Psalmist meant when he said, "Thou gavest commandment to save me." Nothing works contrary to the welfare of the Church of God. She may be tossed on many billows and doing "business in great waters" but all things work together for her good. And it is out of her greatest trials that her greatest blessings often come. We mentioned a moment ago how "the lofty mountains", or God's attributes, bring peace to His people; but the Psalm also speaks of "the little hills" which by righteousness — or by God's wise ordering — shall do the same. All things, small and great, combine in securing the safety and welfare of those who are heirs of salvation. We are told, for example, that the stars in their courses fought against Sisera. The forces of the universe were in array against him. Not only so, but God's people are "in league with the stones of the field." The great and the small! To give another example, the book of Esther is a solemn commentary on how the wheel of providence may turn both to nullify the designs of the wicked and to preserve the righteous. And it all began in such a small way. We read that the king could not sleep. And to beguile the time and compose his mind he asked that a book might be read to him. The book that was brought to his bedside was the right book. It was opened at the right page and at the right moment! On that simple incident the wheel of providence revolved till the enemies of the Church were brought low and God's remnant given a day of joy. "No weapon that is formed against thee shall prosper, and every tongue that shall rise against thee in judgment thou shalt condemn. This is the heritage of the servants of the Lord and their righteousness is of me, saith the Lord." The days in which we live are laden with peril for the world, but He, under Whose control are all things, is the Guardian and the Shepherd of Israel. Though earthly mountains may be cast into the depths of the sea, the God of Jacob shall remain the refuge of His own people for evermore.

Let me say one other thing. Throughout the Bible we read that **the Lord is round about His people not only personally, but through an angelic ministry.** This is something which we should always emphasise. "The chariots of God are twenty thousand, even thousands of angels. The Lord is among them as in Sinai, in the holy place." How sweet it is to sleep with the great promises of Psalm 91 as our pillow:

> "No plague shall near thy dwelling come
> No ill shall thee befall,
> For thee to keep in all thy ways
> His angels charge He shall."

But our safety is not, in the highest sense, dependent on any creature. Our hope and trust rest wholly on the Angel of the Covenant, the Lord Jesus Christ.

Let me conclude my remarks by reminding those who are strangers to God that in the presence of all the storms which are soon to rock our world there is no place to hide. And do you ever think of the day when we must all appear before the Judgment Seat of Christ, and when the Christless shall be driven by the wind of God's displeasure from His presence for ever? May God give you the wisdom to say, "I flee unto Thee to hide me." Christ is now on the Throne of Grace. He is waiting to be gracious. He is speaking to you personally — "How often would I gather you." And if you come, a song shall be born in your heart that shall never die.

> "In shadow of Thy wings I'll joy,
> For Thou my help hast been."

Then, and only then, shall you rejoice in this promise. "As the mountains are round about Jerusalem, so the Lord is round about his people from henceforth even for ever."   Amen.

VII

THE BRIDE'S PRAYER

"Awake, O north wind: and come thou south; blow
upon my garden that the spices thereof may flow
out. Let my beloved come into his garden, and
eat of his pleasant fruits. I am come into my
garden, my sister, my spouse."

(Songs. Ch. 4 : v. 16 and Ch. 5 : v. 1.)

There are seasons in the life of God's people when their souls
cleave to the dust, and when the shadow of spiritual decline may
lie heavily over their spirits. At such times they seek "a little
reviving in their bondage," and, in the words of the Psalm, they
ask the Lord to quicken them according to His word. And when
the Lord draws near to them, and breathes upon them with the
warm breath of His mouth, not only are their own hearts revived
but their prayers also ascend to God that He might visit all His
people with a time of refreshing and with a day of His power.
This, we think, is the way the Church prays here. "Blow upon
my garden." Then she goes on to plead that He would visit His
own garden everywhere and that both His gracious presence and
the fruits of the Spirit might rejoice and encourage waiting
people everywhere. In making a comment on these words let us
consider:

I. The Prayer and its Plea

This prayer, we believe, is for the awakening power of the
Holy Spirit. Under this figure the Spirit of God, in His saving
operations, is often brought before us in the written Word. "The
wind bloweth where it listeth, and thou hearest the sound thereof
but canst not tell whence it cometh or whither it goeth: so is
every one that is born of the Spirit." When God's prophet stood
helpless before the valley of dry bones God commanded him to
pray for the living breath. "Come from the four winds, O breath,
and breathe upon these slain that they may live." It was as "a
rushing mighty wind" that He descended on the Church on the
day of Pentecost. So mighty was His power on that day that the

holy repercussions of the Spirit's descent are still felt in this world, and shall be to the end of time.

The immediate situation which moved the Church to utter this prayer was her awareness of the spiritual decay which had spread over God's vineyard everywhere. In the words of the prophet death had come up into her windows and had entered her palaces. In his own day Isaiah speaks of the ominous stillness, the dark symptom of spiritual death, which everywhere prevailed. "There is none that calleth upon Thy name, that stirreth up himself to lay hold upon Thee". Spiritual silence and sleep always go together. It is when we sleep that Satan, "the boar out of the forest" plays havoc with God's vine. It is then that the enemy sows his tares in the field. The Church knew that when the enemy, through the neglect of those who should keep watch upon the walls of Zion, came in like a flood only the Spirit of the Lord could arrest his power. Therefore she prays, "Awake, O north wind and come thou south."

In the presence of such a state of decline the Church is aware of her own helplessness. There is so much that men can do. They can initiate unspiritual, and often unscriptural, movements within the visible Church, but it is not by might or by power on the part of man that God's cause is rescued and revived but by His Spirit. The question was asked of old "By whom shall Jacob arise for he is small?" "Lord thou knowest." The prophet could see the Church in his own day drawing, as it were, its last breath, and only by a miracle of divine power could Jacob arise again. By proclaiming the word of the Lord the prophet Ezekiel brought all the dry bones of the house of Israel together. They even assumed the appearance and order of life, but as yet there was no breath in them. There was much stir and noise. There was a form of godliness, but no power at all. Only when the prophet, at God's command, prophesied unto the breath did they arise to newness of life. When, conscious of his helplessness, he combined his pleading with earnest supplication did the miracle of a spiritual resurrection happen. It is comparatively easy to assemble men and women together, to assume a religious complexion and to create noise and stir in the religious world; but without the Spirit it can avail, little or nothing.

There was something else of which the Church was aware. She knew that only the Holy Spirit could give its proper exercise to the grace which lodges within the souls of believers. The Holy Spirit is given to God's people as the Spirit of grace and of supplication. But there are seasons when they are at ease in Zion, and when they "rest on their lees." But "woe to them that are at ease in Zion." Her earnest prayer, therefore, was that with the coming of the wind "the spices" of grace in the hearts of God's people might flow forth in continual prayer to God that "in a day of small things" He might arise and plead His own Cause.

It is encouraging to observe how in other days the prayers and conscious helplessness of the Church coincided with mighty displays of God's power. It was often when the Church was on her knees that her Lord went forth in His chariots of salvation and His right hand performed "terrible things". Look at her in Egypt under sentence of death. But she was not silent. "I have surely seen," said the Lord to Moses, "the afflictions of my people who are in Egypt and I have heard their cry . . . and I am come down to deliver them." Their sighs went before their songs — their night of weeping preceded their morning of joy. The wind which dried up the sea before her was the evidence of His saving power. He came in answer to her prayers. Her deliverance out of the bondage of Babylon answered to the same pattern. There they sat and wept as they thought of Zion in her desolation. There they wrestled with God that He might pluck His hand from His bosom and save them. Then it happened. "When the Lord turned again the captivity of Zion we were like them who dream. Then was our mouth filled with laughter."

Look also at what happened in Europe during the midnight darkness of the papal age. Throughout those long years of spiritual decay and death God's "hidden ones" were crying to Him to visit His own desolate vineyard with a day of power, Then the wind began to blow, driving before it the idolatries, superstitions and blasphemies of the papal system which had for so long ensnared and defiled the nations of Europe. God's vineyard was again revived and purified. The Church of the Reformation — the perfect counterpart of the apostolic Church — was born, never to die.

Do we not at this hour live in "a day of small things"? But with all its terrors, lawlessness and apostasy the Lord has still many people in the world whose prayer is that His Kingdom might come and His cause be uplifted. We believe that the day will come when the knowledge of the Lord shall cover the earth as the waters cover the sea. Many today have this same prayer on their lips and in their heart — "Awake O north wind and come thou south." And what is the promise? "When the Lord shall build up Zion, He shall appear in His glory. He will regard the prayer of the destitute and not despise their prayer."

In this prayer there is a just recognition that a true awakening is accompanied by both sorrow and joy. The north wind, we

believe, is typical of the Spirit's work in convincing men of their
sin. "When He is come He will convince the world of sin and of
righteousness and of judgment." He brings the sinner to the bar
of God's Word where he sees that he is without God and without
hope in the world. There also he sees that all his righteousnesses
are as filthy rags and that at the bar of His just judgment he
cannot but bow his head and plead guilty before Him. He also
looks to Him whom he has pierced, and mourns. He mourns over
the fact that he hated Him without a cause. When this strong
wind blows through our souls we are left with nothing but our
sin and its shame.

There have sometimes been so-called "revivals" from which
this godly sorrow was absent, and too often they bore no lasting
fruit. There are those who, like Bunyan's Pliable, receive the word
with a false joy only to return to their old haunts and environment. But true believers have their seasons of sorrow before their
time of love and their hour of deliverance. Before their Bethel
comes their Bochim. We agree that there are different degrees of
this in the experience of God's people but repentance unto life is
a saving grace and can never be divorced from grief over sin.
Let me give an illustration of this. One of the most genuine
revivals that ever took place in our land had this wholesome
characteristic. On one occasion over seven thousand people
gathered in a small picturesque Highland valley to hear the
Gospel. At the end of the day, and as the last Psalm was being
sung, only the preacher and the two leaders of the praise were
able to sing. What had happened to the rest? God's Spirit like a
mighty wind had swept over them. Arrows from the King's bow
had pierced through many hearts. God had convinced them that
they were sinners under wrath. Apart from their weeping they
were silent. But the warm south wind of His grace, love and
forgiveness soon brought them into a state of joy. They were
given a new summer and a new song.

The Church herself could tell the story of that hour when she
passed from death to life. "My beloved spake and said unto me,
Rise up my love, my fair one and come away; for the winter is
past, the rain is over and gone; the flowers appear on the earth,
the time of the singing of birds is come." The winter of sin, with
its snell north wind, had given place to a new and everlasting
summer. The warm wind of His love now wafted through her
soul.

You notice that there was another great reason why the Church
prayed for the reviving breath of the Spirit. It was that Christ's
presence might be known and felt within His own vineyard or

Church. "Let my beloved come into His garden." The power of
the Spirit and the presence of the Lord always go together. There
may be many choice flowers in the garden; but it is Christ, the
Rose of Sharon and the Lily of the Valleys, who gives grace and
fragrance to His own vineyard.

> "That I thy power may behold,
>   and brightness of thy face,"

was the prayer of one who knew that without God's presence in
His own Church there could be only weakness and darkness. The
greatest chastisement that the Lord can bring upon us in this
life is to withdraw His presence from His Church, or, in the wider
sphere, to become a stranger in the land. It is true that the believer may have, like Moses on the Mount, a personal enjoyment
of God's presence while He may become a stranger within the
visible Church. Do we mourn, then, over His absence in those
places of which it could be said in other days that "the Lord was
there"? The Church had that measure of spiritual discernment
which enabled her to differentiate between His presence in the
means of grace and the means of grace without His presence.
Her cry: "Saw ye Him whom my soul loveth?" is the proof of
this. In our worship we may be satisfied with ourselves and with
one another while He may be absent. But it is His presence among
us that lends solemnity and sweetness to the public means of
grace. It is through His presence and power that the dead are
raised and that sinners are converted unto Him.

Once I was present at a prayer meeting in a certain church.
God truly was among us. After the benediction was pronounced
a good woman present gently asked the presiding minister if we
could still tarry there. But we had to part, for here we have but
the tabernacle of a wayfaring man. Do we know what this means?
Have we truly the spiritual discernment to know when He is
present in, or is absent from, His garden. A few years ago a
certain lady visited the North of Scotland. During her sojourn
there she worshipped in a number of congregations where sound
scriptural preaching was proclaimed from each pulpit. But she
entered one church, and as soon as she sat in the pew she could
say, "the Lord is in this place". It was this that endeared that
place to her soul in after days. It was to her a season of heaven
on earth.

Let us plead with Him that He might once again visit those
parts of His vineyard where He is now a stranger. When we read,
for example, of other days in places like our native Highlands,
where men like Dr John Macdonald, Mr Hector MacPhail, "Big"
John MacRae, Dr John Kennedy, Alexander Stewart, and many

others, once reaped such a great harvest, we can only pray:
"To these long desolations Thy feet lift, do not tarry."
Without His power and presence among us the vineyard and the
fruitful field may become dry parched land. O, then let us seek
to discover and disown those sins which have grieved His Spirit
and alienated His gracious presence from our midst.

Now you will notice that after such gracious visitations the
Church is not ashamed to ask her Lord to come into His own
garden. She has ample fare to set before Him. "Let Him eat of
His pleasant fruits." These words mean that where the Spirit is
present His fruits are to be seen in the lives of those whom He
blesses and among whom He works. This is what satisfies, or is
pleasing to, the Lord. The fruits of the Spirit cannot be concealed
in the lives of those who bear them. "But the fruit of the Spirit
is love, joy, peace, longsuffering, gentleness, goodness, faith,
meekness, temperance — against such there is no law." To this
end Christ has chosen and ordained all His people. "I have chosen
you and ordained that ye should go and bring forth fruit and that
your fruit should remain." The Church is God's vineyard or
garden, and each believer is His planting. His people are the
subjects of His care, love and interest. "What could have been
done more for my vineyard that I have not done in it?" Do these
spiritual fruits show themselves in our lives? How ought we to
bow our heads in God's presence as we see our own barrenness
and spiritual dilatoriness. This grief was in the heart of the
Church when she said: "They have made me a keeper of the
vineyards, but my own vineyard have I not kept." We who are
Christian ministers, Christian elders and witnesses are all pro-
fessedly interested in the preservation, purity and increase of
God's cause. And yet through our neglect and prayerlessness
our own lives, our own homes, our own congregations, may fall
under the shadow of spiritual decline. Is it not so? Are our lives
pleasing to God? He comes for fruit, but we have little to show.
This truly is often the grief of the gracious soul. But while we
mourn over our own leanness and the low state of His cause we
hope and long for the day when, through the outpouring of God's
Spirit, the wilderness shall again blossom as the rose.

We mentioned some of the fruits of the Spirit which show
themselves in the true Christian life, but there are others also.
Our Lord Himself spoke of other spiritual fruits which His people
bear. Where does he begin? "Blessed are the poor in spirit for
their's is the Kingdom of Heaven. Blessed are they that mourn
for they shall be comforted. Blessed are the meek, for they shall
inherit the earth. Blessed are they who do hunger and thirst after

righteousness for they shall be filled." If this cluster of blessings is found in our lives then the Lord is with us and dwells in our heart as in a garden. "With this man will I dwell, even with him who is of a poor and a contrite heart and who trembles at My Word." O, dear friends, do we not long for the day when our garden shall be His entirely, or when our souls shall be for ever delivered from all that is of self and of sin? But consider now:

II. **The Lord's Answer to Her Prayer:** "I am come into my garden, my sister, my spouse."

As she would provide Him with the pleasant fruits of His own Spirit, He comes to her laden with blessings. Christ never visits His Church or the soul of the believer empty-handed. He comes to furnish our table. And if the gifts are precious, the presence of the Giver is what lends sweetness to each one. The blessings mentioned here are the choice fare of the heavenly Canaan. The fulness which He communicates to His Church resides in Himself. Here we have the sincere milk of the Word, the wine of His love, the honeycomb of His promises. These all carry the pure aroma of Heaven. In the written Word we have the ecstatic testimonies of those who had tasted of these blessings. "Thy words were found and I did eat them; and Thy word was unto me the joy and rejoicing of mine heart." "More to be desired are they than gold, yea than much fine gold: sweeter also than honey and the honeycomb." "Thy love is better than wine." "O, taste and see that the Lord is good." These indeed are enjoyments, the nature of which it is impossible to describe. Only by personal participation in them can we know their unspeakable sweetness.

We once heard a story of a boy who lived a primitive life in a heathen land. The missionary working among the tribe presented this lad one day with some sweets. He had never seen or tasted such things before. He ran home and told the others about what he had in his hand and in his mouth! They plied him with questions, but he had no words which could describe his enjoyment. At last he said: "Here, you must taste it yourselves."

This enjoyment of the Church was "under the tongue" or in her heart while she was still on her pilgrimage journey. She had in this world of time the earnest of good things to come. And if our blessings here are mixed with many bitter herbs these only increase our longings for that full and eternal enjoyment of God which awaits us at the table above where all tears shall be wiped away from our eyes.

If the Giver and His gifts are so desirable so is His welcome to partake of His feast. "Eat, O friends, drink, yea drink abundantly,

O beloved." He who supplies all our needs and who has in Himself an infinite fulness of grace and truth would have us eat abundantly. Sometimes the public means of grace may be destitute of the spiritual nourishment we require. We cry with David— "Oh that one would give me drink of the water of the well of Bethlehem which is by the gate!" But when, like David's mighty men, our graces are in exercise, we often break through every barrier and overcome the sins which would deprive us of the needed blessing. When prayer, faith and patience do their perfect work, the Lord extends the royal sceptre of His promise to our souls. "What is thy request and what is thy desire?" We are led into his banqueting house where we say with the Psalmist — "A day in thy courts is better than a thousand."

In these days when we see not our signs, our only hope is to plead with God that He might once again stir up His strength and send His Spirit both to arrest the flood of evil and to revive us in the midst of the years. In such a day our silence is our greatest sin. If we open our mouth wide in holy longings, He, on His side, will open the windows of heaven and pour us out a blessing so that there shall not be room enough to receive it. And if we fail in our duty let us remember what is written — "I shall yet be enquired of by the house of Israel to do it for them." May the Lord give us the grace to continue instant in prayer.

VIII

THE SHEPHERD AND HIS FLOCK

"He shall feed his flock like a shepherd." (Isaiah 40 : 11)
Since these words obviously refer to the Lord Jesus Christ in His
tender and constant care toward His people, an introduction to
them is hardly necessary. There are three words in our text on
which I should like to dwell this morning. They are the
"shepherd", the "flock" and the "feeding". Let us consider these.

I: **The Shepherd.**

Christ is before us in the written Word under many glorious
names. Each of these carries its own heavenly fragrance, for "His
name is as ointment poured forth". To all who believe on His
name He is truly precious under whatsoever name the Holy Spirit
brings Him before them in His Word. And there can be few of
His names more endearing to His people than this one. How often,
for example, are our affections moved by the words of the Psalm:
"The Lord is my shepherd". The Father Himself addresses Him
under this name. "Awake, O sword, against my shepherd, and
against the man that is my fellow, saith the Lord of Hosts." And
this is the name by which He brought Himself so often before
His people in the days of His humiliation here. "I am the good
shepherd: the good shepherd giveth his life for the sheep."
In the Epistle to the Hebrews he is designated as **"that great
Shepherd of the sheep"**. And wherein does His greatness consist?
He is, in His Person and Being, the Eternal Son of God equal to
the Father and to the Holy Spirit both in power and glory. All the
attributes of the Godhead belong to Him in their unchanging fullness and perfection. He is the ever-living "I am". This is how He
spoke of Himself while He was in this world. "Before Abraham
was, I am." Those — and there are many such in this day of
blasphemy and unbelief — who would reduce Him to the level
of a mere man have to contend with the witness of God Himself
on this claim.
It was, indeed, necessary that He who was to redeem us to God
should be equal to God Himself. Sin brought such dishonour
upon the glory and majesty of God that He could never accept
satisfaction or atonement from any being lower than Himself.
That Christ was in no respect lower than God in His Being is,

to give one instance, clearly shown by God Himself where He speaks of Him "my Fellow" or "mine equal". Only He could satisfy Divine justice, endure the penalty of a broken law and of a violated covenant. Only He could or would endure the stroke of that sword which the justice of God must inflict upon Him as the surety and substitute of His people. Only God could break the dread sway of sin, and put it away for ever. Only He could have borne the burden of imputed sin which would, otherwise, have crushed and destroyed all humanity for ever. When He entered this world, therefore, in our nature, He took all the perfections of Deity with Him. He was "Emmanuel, God with us".

It was necessary also that He who was to suffer and die must also be man. It was man who sinned and God the Father could not therefore in justice lay the penalty of sin on one who was not also a true man. He took our nature that in our nature He might die — the just in the room of the unjust. It is the infinite greatness of the Person which lends dignity, efficacy and glory to His finished work of redemption.

In the Gospel our Lord speaks also of Himself as **"The good Shepherd"**. What the Church, both in Heaven and on earth, sees in His coming into the world to die for her is the greatness of His love. He loved all His people with an everlasting love. Why He loved us we cannot tell. We sinned against Him. We hated Him without a cause. We despised and rejected Him. We nailed Him to the tree and put Him to open shame; but in spite of all this He loved us to the end. "Greater love hath no man than this that a man should lay down His life for his friends". But, as we were by nature, we were not His friends but His enemies. Only when He changed our hearts, and gave us the spirit of repentance, did we become His friends. O! the wonder of His love as we see it in contrast to all our ill-deservings. Is it any wonder that the theme of the songs of the redeemed in the heavenly world should be: "Unto Him who loved us and washed us from our sins in His own blood"? As in the case of Paul who spoke of himself as "the chief of sinners", each one of His people puts himself or herself in the same category and shall wonder, through all eternity, at the love which embraced them and rescued them.

And how thankful we should be that this love is united to infinite power. "All power is given unto me in heaven and on earth." Satan "the son of mischief" took all humanity out of the hand of the first Adam. We all sinned in him and fell with him in his first transgression. But Satan can never take any of God's elect out of Christ's hand. "I give them eternal life, and they shall never perish neither shall any man pluck them out of mine hand."

They are kept by the power of God. On the great day He shall give an account to the Father of all for whom He died. "Behold I and the children whom God hath given me." Satan's power is great; so is the power of sin, but Christ's power, love and faithfulness stand between us and all that would destroy us.

God's word also speaks of our Lord as **"The chief Shepherd"** of His sheep. "And when the chief Shepherd shall appear ye shall receive a crown of glory that fadeth not away."

On the natural level there are some who leave their flocks under the care of their servants. The sheep belong to them; but they give them no personal attention. Some, indeed, would consider it beneath their dignity to attend personally to their flocks. Now Christ, as the Head of the Church and the King of Zion, has ordained and appointed angels and men to care for His flock in this lower vale. Angels are ministering spirits who are sent forth to minister to those who are heirs of salvation. They watch over them night and day. They keep them in all their ways. The Lord also has chosen men who care for the spiritual welfare of His people. Peter, after his profession of love to Christ, was commanded to feed His sheep and lambs. Such men should manifest their love to Christ by their love to His people. The Lord has a called, converted and devoted ministry within His Church on earth who attend to the spiritual needs of His people. But, however faithful and loving all such may be, the Lord does not, in the highest sense, leave His people under their care. He Himself is **the chief Shepherd.** When Moses was offered an angel to lead God's Israel through the great and terrible wilderness into the place of their rest, he said: "If thy presence go not with me carry us not up hence." Under God's hand he was a shepherd himself, and he knew the value of angelic protection and care, but only under the wings of the Eternal would he feel safe. Under the pillar of cloud by day and of fire by night would he know that no harm could befall them. Above and beyond all that man and angels could do was His own unfailing care. How sweet to the believing soul are those Psalms which speak of this.

> "But his own people like to sheep
> thence to go forth He made.
> And he amidst the wilderness
> them, as a flock did lead."

> "Thy foot he'll not let slide, nor will
> He slumber that thee keeps,
> Behold he that keeps Israel
> He slumbers not, nor sleeps."

We seek, as we ought to do, to keep ourselves unspotted from the world and, by His grace, to persevere in the way of His commandments. This is the desire and resolve of God's people. But while all the people of God ever strive to do so, their faith rests on Him who alone is the Keeper of Israel: for they know that without Him they could do nothing. It was this that gave such unspeakable comfort to the Psalmist. "Thou shalt guide me with thy counsel and afterward receive me to glory."

Think also of the **sympathy and love of the Shepherd** toward His flock. In the natural world the shepherd, however tender and faithful, cannot understand how the weary or enfeebled sheep or lamb may feel in the way. There may be a hidden instinctive pain of which the shepherd can know nothing. This is so because they belong to two different dimensions of existence. There is a fundamental difference of nature. Our Lord, however, has a human nature as well as the Divine. He is, therefore, touched with a feeling of our infirmities. "In all their afflictions He was afflicted." In this world He was a man of sorrows and acquainted with grief. Surely He hath borne our griefs and carried our sorrows." His sympathy with His afflicted people is, therefore, very real. He has passed through all our sorrows. Although in Him was no sin, all our weaknesses, perplexities, trials and hidden griefs were in His cup. Our tears and our wounded spirits touch Him as they cannot touch our nearest friends on earth. His people are the apple of His eye. He knows our frame. He knows our enemies. He knows our burdens. He also knows that many of our sufferings are due to our attachment to Him, and to His cause in this world. "For thy sake are we killed all the day, we are accounted as sheep for the slaughter." One wonder of His care over us is the way He adapts Himself to our personal states. He leadeth gently those that are with young. He carries the lambs to His bosom. He applies His balm to the hurts of those who suffer for His sake. When they are ready to halt He gives them rest. "As a beast goeth down into the valley the Spirit of the Lord caused them to rest; so didst thou lead thy people to make thyself a glorious name." (Is. 63). How sweet to know then that nothing will ever emerge in our lives but He is ever beside each one of us. "The Lord is my shepherd." "I will fear no evil for Thou art with me."

The next word in our text that we would look at is:

II. The Flock

The Lord speaks in His Word of His people here as "a little flock". Some think that this phrase is a term of endearment. And so it is. But it is also a word which enables us to see that, in comparison to the rest of the world, the Lord's people have often, if not always, been small in number. There have been times when they were few, feeble and hidden. Although the Lord — and we should bless His name for it — has much people in the world today — they are still, compared to the teeming masses of humanity, "a very small remnant." But they are the salt of the earth. It is for the Elect's sake that God bears with us. For their sake He shortens the days of anguish. In the ultimate sense, however, those who make up Christ's flock are not a small number. They are "a great multitude which no man could number." When Abraham, at God's command, looked at the stars of heaven He said to him, "so shall thy seed be". And we know that all the stars which grace the universe are known only to God. They are in their number utterly beyond human calculation. We believe also that the day is coming when God's people shall make the earth resound with His praise. He is going to bring His sons from afar and His daughters from the ends of the earth till, among Jew and Gentiles, the knowledge of the Lord shall cover the earth as the waters cover the sea.

But coming nearer to our theme we ask a question. How may we identify His people in this world? What are their peculiar marks? The Lord's people may differ in many ways within the context of their individual Christian experience, but they have also so many things in common. For one thing they all love the Lord Who redeemed them. Whatever their own feelings and fears if they are His, His love is shed abroad in their hearts by the Holy Spirit who dwells in them. "Whom having not seen, ye love." "The righteous love thee." Peter, newly out of the devil's sieve, and still under a cloud of fear and shame, could say, "Lord, Thou knowest that I love Thee." The flood of the adversary could not extinguish that flame of love to Christ which beamed through his spirit. We are not always conscious of our love to Christ. It is often a hidden grace which shows itself in other ways.

The evidence of their love to Him is really seen in their spiritual discernment and obedience. They know the Shepherd's voice. To the Church in the Song of Solomon Christ's voice had no counterpart in Heaven or on earth. "The voice of my beloved." "No man ever spake like this man." "Cause me", was the prayer of David, "to hear thy voice for in Thee do I trust." They say that, naturally speaking, sheep can distinguish between the voice of the shepherd and all other voices. The imitation of his voice may be almost perfect; but the false voice never deceives them.

God's true people listen only to God's Word. The false shepherd — and there are many such in our day — whose voice deviates from God's Word — they ignore and reject. This has often involved them in sufferings and death. Throughout the long day of historical time many of them suffered for their devotion to Christ and His Word. Rather than forsake His Word, or leave the way of holiness and truth, many of them chose and welcomed death.

Not only are they bound to the way, but their hearts are also bound to those who are with them in the way. How beautifully is this seen, for example, in the life of Ruth as she said an everlasting farewell to her people and her gods. "Whither thou goest, I will go; thy people shall be my people and thy God my God." The love of Bunyan's pilgrims for the way was of a part with their love to Christ and to one another. God was their companion and guide. And they had fellowship with Him and with one another both in their joys and sorrows. A good Christian girl was once on the eve of leaving her home for one of our Scottish cities. She was concerned as to where she could find true Christian fellowship and food for her soul. At the Throne of Grace she addressed the Lord in these words: "Tell me, O thou whom my soul loveth, where thou feedest, where thou makest thy flock to rest at noon." When she arrived in the city she sat on the Sabbath evening in a certain Church, and great was her astonishment when the minister preached from these very words. There her soul found rest and nourishment for many days.

Another mark which is peculiar to the flock of God is that they are reconciled to the Lord's hand when He brings them under the rod of correction. If sheep are often foolish and apt to go astray so are the Lord's people sometimes. If they heed not His voice which says, "This is the way, walk ye in it", they may come under His loving chastisement. But, however sore these trials, He will not give them over to death. "The Lord hath me chastised sore, but not to death given over."

Satan may at times insinuate that His chastisements are not the tokens of His love but of His displeasure. But He gives them the needed grace whereby they are able to "hear the rod" and Him who appoints it. Not till we reach our heavenly home shall we see the wisdom and love of God in the ordering of His providence. Can we not even now, with so much of our Christian life in retrospect, thank Him for the use of His rod when we were apt to go astray into the way of danger?

Let us now say a word on:

III. The Feeding

The great end for which Christ came into the world was that His flock might have life and have it more abundantly. He who is their resurrection out of a state of spiritual death is also their sustaining life. Of His fulness they all receive and grace for grace. As sheep, naturally, are clean creatures, the Lord's people, as new creatures in Christ, are conscious of new desires which only God can satisfy. The evidence of their regeneration is that they hunger and thirst after righteousness. Reclaimed and redeemed from the "far country" of sin, they no longer desire the husks which graceless men and women live on. They have for ever left the impoverished and unclean fare of a degenerate world. Their Shepherd has furnished their table with the wholesome food and drink of the heavenly Canaan.

When God brought His people out of Egypt He gave them manna from heaven and water out of the smitten rock. And the spiritual Israel feed on the pastures of His Word. The Word of God is their life in every age. "Thy words were found and I did eat them." It is by "the sincere milk of the Word" that His lambs are nourished. His people confess that "His mouth is most sweet". It is, in other words, through the channel of His Word, that He communicates His grace to their souls. The words which He speaks to them are life and truth. Exercised Christians read the Word and love to hear it expounded in the public means of grace. God says to them each day: "Arise and eat because the journey is too great for thee."

Inseparable from this pasture is the practice of prayer. "Give us this day our daily bread." "Evermore give us this bread." God did not bring the manna into the houses of the Israelites. Nor did He place it in their mouth. They had to go out into the fields and gather it. Ruth had to glean on the fields of Boaz for her daily bread. Those who neglect the means of grace God will not bless. Family worship and public worship go together. If the one is persistently neglected the other becomes an empty formality. There are those who say that they can worship God in their homes without going to His House, but in so saying they dishonour God. We are to keep His Sabbaths and reverence His sanctuary. But God's children have also secret dealings with the Lord in prayer. It is in the secret place that they often enjoy more of His presence, and that He supplies their needs according to His riches in Christ. In all the means of grace they open their mouth in prayer and desire, and He fills it. They extend the hand of faith toward Him and He gives them a token for good.

We mentioned how the Lord uses His rod of chastisement for their safety; and does He not also feed them on bitter herbs, and give them the waters of Marah to drink? There are seasons when instead of bread to eat they are given tears of sorrow. The cup which He puts to their mouth is not always sweet. The sorrows of the flock come from many sources. "In this world ye shall have tribulation." But it only lasts "for a small moment". Soon, very soon, He shall wipe all tears from their eyes. There are no bitter herbs, no waters of Marah, in Heaven. Sorrow and sighing shall for ever flee away. "And now ye have sorrow, but I shall see you again and your heart shall rejoice and your joy no man taketh from you."

Dear friend, do you know the Lord as your shepherd? Do you bear the marks of His own? Do you feed at their table? Let me end my remarks with a little story. It is that of a well-trained elocutionist who once at the request of some friends repeated the twenty-third Psalm. So impressed were many by his art that when he finished there was the sound of subdued, and respectful applause. In that company there was an elderly Christian man who also, in a halting and broken voice — and not without much feeling — repeated the Psalm. When he finished some were in tears. "How is it," someone asked the master of elocution, "that when you repeated the Psalm some applauded but none wept; but when the other repeated it he brought tears to our eyes?" His answer was, "The difference between us is this: I know the Psalm, but he knows the Shepherd." My friend you also knew the Psalm from your mother's knee, perhaps. But do you know the Shepherd? "And this is life eternal that they might know thee, the only true God, and Jesus Christ whom thou hast sent."

IX

THE HEAVENLY FORETASTE

"Now faith is the substance of things hoped for, the evidence of things not seen." (Heb. II : 1).

In these words we have a perfect definition of the grace of faith. True faith is God's gift, and it is begotten in the soul by the Spirit of God. All men may have some kind of faith, but all men have not the faith which rests on Christ alone for salvation, and which, whatever the trials in the way, brings the soul to Heaven. Saving faith is a grace which the hand of the Heavenly Father has planted in the soul of the renewed man. It thrives and matures to the extent in which it is exercised in relation to the Lord and His Word. Both the written Word, and the Personal Word — the Lord Jesus — are the proper foundation, life, and objects of saving faith. We must, therefore, never confuse ordinary, rational, historical, or even theological faith, with the faith, which, in union with the living Head in Heaven, is the substance of things hoped for. Let us think then, for a moment, of:

I. The Things which God's People Hope for:

The "things" mentioned in the verse do not, of course, come within the category of "things seen". "For what a man sees why doth he yet hope for it." "We look not", says the apostle, "at the things which are seen, but at the things which are not seen." In other words this faith has a far reaching vision which sees, or apprehends, things beyond the visible and temporal order, or even beyond space and time. It apprehends the things which are spiritual and eternal. A supernatural grace, it brings the blessings of "the heavenly places" into the hearts of true believers while they are still sojourning in this lower world. Some of the things hoped for by those who have this precious faith are mentioned in the immediate context.

The context reminds us, for example, that all true Christians hope for the fulfilment of all the Divine promises, which "by faith and patience" they shall inherit at last. The promises of God are not only great and precious, but in their variety and number we cannot fully describe or reckon them. (Ps. 40). Like the stars which fill the night sky, their number is known only to God.

Some of His promises relate to our requirements, trials and comforts in this broken life. These come within the sweep of God's Covenant love and care, as expressed in the words, "I will never leave thee nor forsake thee." As our needs arise, and our trials come and go, we see the Lord daily fulfilling His Word in providing grace for the journey which, otherwise, is "too great" for us.

The large majority of the promises, however, can only be inherited in Heaven with God. The streams of daily mercy and grace communicated through the promises of God here, shall at last give way to a full and perfect realisation of all that we hoped for in this life.

We read in this chapter, that one of the things which all the people of God hoped for in the past was the promise of "a city which hath foundations". He gave this promise to Abraham. It was the promise of Heaven. In all his pilgrimage, therefore, he sought that city which, by faith, he saw as through a glass. The view that he enjoyed of that good land "wherein dwelleth righteousness" led him to confess that he was a stranger in the earth. Both his heart and walk were, from the day that God called him out of the world, bent towards the heavenly country, the land of his desire. God convinced him that here he had no continuing city. Man, indeed, is destined to outlive the physical universe, but only the Heaven-born man acts on that knowledge by seeking a dwelling-place with God. "But now they desire a better country, that is an heavenly; wherefore God is not ashamed to be called their God, for He hath prepared for them a city." To that longed-for Home God will bring His people. "He led them forth by the right way that they may go to a city of habitation." (Ps. 107). Our glorified Lord is now in that city of many mansions, preparing a place for His chosen and redeemed people. Do we not associate our sweetest earthly joys with the word "Home"? It is so spiritually. Home is where our loved ones reside. And Heaven is the palace of the Great King, our Father in Christ, who has begotten us to Himself. Our beloved Redeemer is also there. So is our Mystical Mother, the "Jerusalem which is from above" or "the Church of the first-born written in Heaven". There the whole family of God will meet at last to enjoy the pleasures which are at His right hand for evermore.

But again, God's redeemed people hope also that the Lord will fit them to enjoy Heaven with Himself. Reconciled by His blood, clothed in His righteousness, regenerated and sanctified by the Spirit, they are made meet to inherit His Kingdom. The many corruptions which still cling to them God will put away.

When they pray for holiness He sometimes answers their prayers "by terrible things in righteousness". (Ps. 65). He brings them through the fires of suffering that in the end they may come forth as purified gold. "Many shall be purified, and made white and tried." This process necessarily precedes the glory that shall be revealed in them. Then shall they "shine as the brightness of the firmament and . . . as the stars for ever and ever." (Dan. 12).

They hope and long also for unbroken communion with God. All their future happiness lies within the promise that they shall see His face and dwell eternally in His presence. In the communication of His love and in the enjoyment of His felt presence the Lord here is often "like a wayfaring man". One day His love flows sweetly through the soul, while the next we seem to dwell in a "thirsty land where there is no water". (Ps. 63). Christian enjoyment has its ebbs and flows. But what is the promise? "We shall be satisfied with the goodness of thy house." In Heaven they shall thirst no more. All divinely planted desires which form the life and content of true Christian hope, God will at last satisfy. "He will fulfil the desire of them that fear Him." (Ps. 145). Heaven is a place where the provisions and consolations of God's covenant love shall surprise and delight us beyond all we ever knew or thought.

Now the hope of these things is not a lovely dreamland, or a species of wishful thinking, which has no foundation in reality. The words hint at:

II. The Evidence of their Existence, and the Certainty of their Enjoyment:

The evidence of these things we have in the infallible Word of God. God's promise of eternal life and happiness to His people is so certain that in order to show its immutability He confirmed it by an oath (Heb. 6-17). "For when God made promise to Abraham, because He could swear by no greater he swore by himself, saying, surely blessing I will bless thee. And so after he had patiently endured he obtained the promise." (Heb. 6 : 15). Every promise made over to the Church of Christ is thus ratified and sealed. One specific reason why the Scriptures are given us is "that we may know that we have eternal life." The inner faith of the believer rests, therefore, on God's testimony in His Word. And when we believe His witness we have the evidence of its absolute certainty in our own souls. Those born of God have this witness in themselves (1 John v). The accents of faith have thus the ring of certainty and assurance. True faith, therefore, is not only theological: it is also experimental. "We know and are

sure that this is the true God and eternal life." Even should our
faith falter at times — during these seasons when darkness and
sorrow descend upon us — yet God remains faithful to His
promise, "for He cannot deny Himself." A frowning providence
may seem at times to stand opposed, or even in contradiction,
to the promise. Like Jacob we say: "Against me are all these
things." But in every storm His Covenant promise remains sure
and steadfast. "The end of the Lord" is always good and kind in
His dealings with His people, and though Heaven and earth shall
pass away His Word can never be broken.

There is, however, another side of our text. Some there are
who give ready assent to the truths of God's word. They accept
and adhere to systems of sound doctrines in all intellectual honesty.
Their minds may have much light, and they may have a sense
of appreciation of the value of the truths cherished. And yet
such people may be quite destitute of the **substance,** or the life,
which these truths should convey to the soul by the Spirit of God.
The Pharisees, for example, had the cold light of truth, but Christ
said to them: "I know you that the love of God is not in you."
Thus faith goes deeper and higher than any acquiescence in a
doctrinal system, however absolutely necessary to our faith such
an acceptance must be. True faith brings the very substance of
what we hope for into our souls. Believers get a "foretaste" on
earth of all their future enjoyments in Heaven. This is what is
called "the earnest" of good things to come. The assurance and
enjoyment of the love of Christ; the peace which reigns in the
conscience through the sprinkling of the blood of atonement; joy
in the Holy Ghost, and communion with God, are the very life
and substance of the things we hope to enjoy in Heaven. Does
not Christ Himself dwell in our hearts by faith? What life and
sweetness did the Bride extract from the promises! Though she
was still on her pilgrimage to Heaven, Christ addressed her in
these words: "Thy lips, O my spouse, drop as the honeycomb;
honey and milk are under thy tongue." (Songs 4). She had in her
heart the very food of Caanan even while she was still in the
desert. The grace of life in the soul is glory in the bud, and Heaven
in miniature. It is the day spring from on high with tokens of the
coming everlasting summer. These enjoyments have their roots
in reality. They are refreshing streams of life from the very Throne
of God. But they are infinitely beyond the reach, or the knowledge,
of those who have only a form of godliness but who know nothing
of its power.

We are not, however, to conclude that the sensible enjoyments
of Christian experience — however sweet and precious — are, in

the matter of faith, of equal value with God's testimony in His Word. No. Faith must often live without its assurance or enjoyment. It must cling to the promise in the days of darkness and destitution. Such days are not, by any means, rare in the history of the Church of God. The disciples on the Mount saw the glory of the Redeemer. They heard the voice out of the cloud. They tasted the powers of the world to come. The very bliss of heaven touched their souls. It was a day in His Courts, which is better than a thousand elsewhere. Such seasons belong to an exercised Christian experience, and are greatly to be prized and sought after. They prove that we are welcome guests at God's table, and that we have "the knowledge of the holy." And yet they are not the foundation of our faith; but that Word which is for ever settled in Heaven. (II Pet. 1). Lastly let me mention:

III. The Infinite Importance of Ascertaining Whether this Faith is our own:

There is, as we hinted a moment ago, a form of faith which consists entirely in an external and nominal profession. For example, the foolish virgins had all the outward exercise and appearance of the wise. They had lamps, but no oil; they had faith without substance. They lacked the life of God in their souls. God puts His treasure in the earthen vessels; but those vessels are renewed by the grace of God, and are therefore "unto honour". The love of Jesus is shed abroad in their hearts. If the love of Christ is shed abroad in our hearts our hope shall never be put to shame. An empty faith may pass the test of time, but not the test of death or judgment. Therefore the lamps of the foolish ones flickered and died in the hour of death. Many, for example, travel to the great eternity sure that if they have a certain ecclesiastical connection, and if they fulfil their several religious duties, then Heaven is sure. Too often we presume that God is pleased with what pleases us. The Immortal Dreamer, John Bunyan, tells us how "Ignorance" went through life and death sure that his "Vain Hope" would take him to Heaven. It was at the door of Heaven that he made the dread, and to him the very surprising, discovery that he was destitute of saving faith. From the pinnacle of presumption he was cast into the depths of perdition. Satan can weave a false hope and a false faith in our soul; but only those who have the Spirit of God can say, "Thou knowest, Lord, that I love thee." Does our faith then rest on what Christ is, what Christ says, and what He did when He died on the tree? Have we experienced the great change of a new birth which all who hope to enter Heaven must know? Can we say that "the Lord our Righteousness" is all our hope, and that we love Him who first loved us? Have we indeed this faith which works by love?

Let each and all of us here today face these solemn questions; and may the Lord enable us to answer them in a way that shall be to His own glory and to the everlasting good of our souls. For the night cometh when no man can work.

X

" LET US NOT SLEEP "

"And that knowing the time, that now it is high time to awake out of sleep; for now is our salvation nearer when we believed." (Rom. XIII : II).

When these words were first written the Church, under the New Testament Dispensation, was still in its spiritual infancy. But even then the Apostle could see a dark cloud of persecution descending upon it. The Dragon was casting a flood out of his mouth that he might devour both the Church of Christ and her seed. The heathen were raging against the Lord and His anointed. Satan's emissaries never tire in their opposition to Christ and to those who serve Him. But the Apostle was aware of another danger. This danger was within the Church itself. It was that the people of God might, in their hour of peril, lose their spiritual vigilance and forget the exhortation that they should always watch and pray. This danger within the Church was, we believe, much greater than any to which she might be exposed from without. Let us offer a word on:

I. The Sin against which we are here warned

"Let us not sleep, as do others."

We can, dear friends, expect nothing from a godless world or from the multitudes who make a dead religious profession but that they should remain in this state of spiritual slumber and death. But the people of God have, in a day of His power, been delivered out of this condition. They are a people whom God has awakened out of their spiritual unconcern. They heard His voice: "Awake thou that sleepest, and arise from the dead and Christ shall give thee light." "And you hath He quickened, who were dead in trespasses and sins." But the danger is that they may sleep again. Needless to say, the true people of God can never return to that state of total spiritual death out of which God has called them. They can never fall out of a state of grace, or lose their souls. In the day of their regeneration Christ gives them eternal life. But while they have grace in their souls, that grace may not always be in exercise. Spiritual slumber may overtake their eyes. The Psalmist prayed against this danger. "Lighten mine eyes, lest I sleep the sleep of death."

Are there not influences abroad in our day which induce this state? Many have, for example, gone to sleep on the lap of their material comforts. They "wax fat" in the enjoyment of temporal favours while they "kick" against their spiritual duties and neglect the Throne of Grace. There are also ensnaring distractions peculiar to this age which too often eat up our time and deaden our souls. Some of these have invaded our very homes.

And the world in which we live, with its deceptive haze of religious formalism, may become an "enchanted ground". When Christian and Hopeful became aware of this danger on their pilgrimage to Heaven they had to stir up one another lest the fatal atmosphere by which they were surrounded, and which so menacingly touched their eyes, should overcome them. How solemnly is this brought before us in the parable of the virgins. If this slumber began with the foolish ones, it did not end with them. It overcame the wise as well. Spiritual sleep, we believe, is infectious. Our Lord predicted that in the latter days the love of many would wax cold. It was here that the sad decline of the Church at Ephesus began. She had forsaken her first love. This was the root cause of her fall. The Lord, however, did not say that the love of all would wax cold, but that the love of many would. How we ought to thank God that there are, throughout the land, the "few names" who do not defile their garments and who keep watch on the walls of Zion!

Many also, as we know, sleep on the lap of a false hope, and many others are lulled into this state by the voice of the false prophet — so common in our age — whose favourite words are, "peace, peace". But the Lord tells us that for such "there is no peace".

We ought to remind ourselves that prayer, whether at the family altar or in the public means of grace, is good and necessary in its own place; but the Lord also commands us to watch as well as to pray. The two go together, and what God has joined together let no man put asunder.

The Church in the Song sought Christ on her bed in the night; but the Psalmist said that He would give no rest to his eyelids, nor go up upon his bed, till he had found a place for the Lord, or till the Lord would return to His Zion, the place where He desired to dwell.

All the people of God have their own infirmities and we make no excuse for these. In the awful crisis of Gethsemane the disciples slept. While the spirit was willing, the flesh was weak. They slept during the hour of danger and of their Lord's agony. But

Satan and all his followers were wide awake. Judas Iscariot was not asleep in that dread hour. "Woe to them that are at ease in Zion." In the days of the prophet Isaiah there was a fatal spiritual stillness within the Church and over which God's prophet mourned. "There is none that calleth upon thy name; that stirreth up himself to take hold of thee: for thou hast hid thy face from us, and hast consumed us because of our iniquities." Was he not an exception? Yes, he was. "And I will wait upon the Lord that hideth his face from the house of Jacob, and I will look for him." These are his words in regard to his own secret exercises before God at the Throne of Grace. May we be like him. Observe also:

II. The Danger and Aggravation of this Sin

"And that knowing the time . . . "

In the world of nature there are seasons when we can relax. A ship — to use an illustration — may be sailing on a calm sea. The wind may be favourable. The sky clear. All is peaceful. But for the Church of God there are no such seasons in this world. For it, the wind is often contrary, and the hour may be dark and perilous. Its enemies in hell and on earth are ever seeking its hurt. There is not a moment in its life here when it should remain listless or discard "the whole armour of God", since all the principalities and powers of the kingdom of darkness seek its destruction. The Christian life is not a sleep but an unceasing warfare and a constant watchfulness.

And are there not times in the history of the Church which call for greater vigilance and greater spiritual activity? The days we live in are laden with danger. Whether we think of the political or ecclesiastical world the same thing is true. These truly are times of peril without parallel in history. The shadow of nuclear devastation is over our planet. And this, we fear, is something that we cannot now escape. There are, we believe, those who have the mind of the Lord in relation to this coming woe. Are we not really paving a way for God's indignation? The very sins for which God, in His fierce anger, destroyed peoples and nations in the past are rearing their ugly heads in our midst and are being condoned and sanctioned by our government, by many Godless men and by some of our so-called Church leaders. This should be one of our deepest sorrows, spiritual concern before God.

You recall that when God told Abraham of his intention to destroy Sodom and Gomorrah he immediately prayed that God would spare these cities should He have a remnant there. He was in the path of duty. With a cloud of wrath over those evil places

Abraham did not go to sleep. And why does His judgment tarry
with us? You remember what is written— "For except the Lord
had left us a very small remnant we should have been as Sodom
and like unto Gomorrah." Another prophet prayed in a later
age that the Lord in the midst of wrath would remember mercy.
Jonah was in the way of disobedience when he slept in the ship.
He had been sent to warn the people of Nineveh, and to pray
that God might give them a spirit of repentance. Instead of doing
this he sought to flee from God's presence and gave way to
slavish fear. Some of us here have seen two generations given over
to the sword. We have witnessed two waves of God's judgment
passing over the nations of Europe. "The second woe is past and,
behold, the third woe cometh quickly." How can we be at ease
in Zion in such an hour?

But there are graver dangers than these potential physical perils.
What of the spiritual realm? What of the cause of Christ in our
day? The time was when "Bethel" could be written on the very
portals of the Reformation Church in Scotland. The Lord was
there. But as it happened in Israel of old "the boar out of the
forest" has broken down her hedges, and the once fruitful vine
whose branches covered our land is now in a state of decay. Not
only so, but there are many men now within her pale whose sole
aim is to bring her under the papal yoke, and into the bondage of
darkness and idolatry out of which God once delivered her.

The process of spiritual degeneration can hardly go further. And
how could such a thing happen? What caused this decay and
decline? It all happened "while we slept". Christ in his parable
of the tares reminds us that the enemy, and those who serve him,
are ever trying to undo God's work. It was "while men slept" —
the men who ought to have kept watch in the night — that the
enemy did his evil work. Look at the Protestant Church in Britain
today. Is it not evident that its ministry is largely graceless or
unconverted, for no man born of God departs from God's word
either into the way of unbelief or into the way of an unscriptural
unity, or as to how God should be worshipped. And ought we
not to mourn over this for it is the outcome of our own spiritual
slumber and that of our fathers with whom, in the words of the
Psalm, we have sinned.

A famous Highland minister, Mr Lachlan Mackenzie, once
made a comment in one of his sermons on Christ when he was
asleep in the ship while, on the other hand, the disciples were
awake and crying to Him for His intervention in their danger.
Neither the roaring sea nor the howling wind wakened Him, but
the prayers of His disciples did. "As long," he said, "as we have

in the Church of God on earth men and women who keep praying to God for the preservation of His cause, the Church, like the Ark in the flood, is safe."

But woe to the Church when its watchmen sleep. The cry of the people of God in such an hour is, "Awake, why sleepest thou, O Lord? Arise; cast us not off for ever. Wherefore hidest thou thy face and forgettest our affliction and our oppression?". As great storms are approaching our world, it is not the roar of war on the billows of His judgment that shall awake Him out of sleep, but the cries or prayers of His people. This is what brought Him down in other days. "I have heard the groanings of my people who are in Egypt. I have seen their affliction and I am come down to save them." When Mordecai saw how the enemies of Israel had decreed their destruction he reminded Queen Esther of her urgent duty, and warned her against remaining silent in such an hour. "For if thou altogether holdest thy peace at this time then shall there enlargement and deliverance arise to the Jews from another place; but thou and thy father's house shall be destroyed". God will have a cause in the world to the end of time, but He has often removed His candlestick out of places which had been highly favoured of Him and transferred it to other places and lands. Why? For the misuse of privilege and the neglect of spiritual duties. O, that the spirit of grace and of supplication might remain with us! If we grieve Him, He may leave us. It is easy to alienate God's presence from our midst, but it is not so easy to bring Him back again. This is one of the solemn lessons before us in God's Word. We know of many places where the Lord once tarried but where He is now a stranger. The cry of the prophet is full of instruction: "O, the hope of Israel, the Saviour thereof in time of trouble, why shouldest thou be as a stranger in the land, and as a wayfaring man that turneth aside to tarry for a night?" There is only one answer to this question. Their own sin and their spiritual unconcern in the presence of many evils had alienated His presence from their midst. Although the Lord shall never utterly forsake His own people in His covenant or in His promise, this denial of His presence and saving power is the greatest chastisement that He can bring upon them in this world. It were well for us if we could say with the Psalmist, "My soul waiteth for the Lord more than they that watch for the morning: I say more than they that watch for the morning." And listen to the voice of His Bride, "Until the day break and the shadows flee away, I will get me to the mountain of myrrh and to the hill of frankincense." These words express the soul exercises of the Church in other days, when, in the way of prayer and patience, she remained on her knees. Notice also :

III. The Duty Urged

"Let us, therefore, cast off the works of darkness, and let us put on the armour of light . . . "

There are garments which are appropriate for the night as there are garments which are suitable for the day. It would be wrong and unbecoming to appear in the day time in the garments which clothe us in the night. And the call of God to His people is to put off their former conversation, or the habits which dominated their lives in the days of their ignorance. As the children of the day, they should discard these forever. All imitation of an ungodly world they should for ever forsake. "And have no fellowship with the unfruitful works of darkness, but rather reprove them." This, we know, is a continuous exercise of soul with God's people The works which they seek to put off would still cling to them so that, in the words of another, they are always beginning. Not till they close their eyes in time shall they be made perfect in holiness.

You notice that as they cast off the works of darkness they put on the armour of light. We are commanded to put on the Lord Jesus Christ and to make no provision for the flesh. As the children of the day, they are in conflict with the powers of darkness, but since they have put on the Lord Jesus Christ no enemy can prevail against them. He is an almighty Saviour. When David went forward to engage the giant of Gath he was not afraid. "I come to thee in the name of the Lord of Hosts, the God of the armies of Israel whom thou hast defied."

The Scriptures speak of the believer as clothed in Christ as his righteousness, his strength, his light and his salvation; but the word which is here used means also those weapons of our spiritual warfare which the apostle mentions in his letter to the Ephesians. And how adequate these are for all those who fight the good fight of faith ! Hell has never forged a weapon, and never shall, which shall overcome God's child if in his armour he be clad, and if these weapons he rightly employs. This is what John Bunyan discovered when, with the Sword of God's Word in his hand, he challenged the great adversary. "Rejoice not against me, O mine enemy: when I fall I shall arise; when I sit in darkness, the Lord shall be a light unto me." "The armour of light." "The Sun of Righteousness." "For the Lord our God is a sun and shield." These words proclaim that while all the graces, all the provisions and promises of God are at the disposal of the Church of Christ in her spiritual warfare and perseverance He is, at the same time, present with her Himself. Therefore, no weapon formed against her shall ever prosper. But the warfare must go on, till we, by God's grace, can say with Paul: "I have fought a good fight; I have finished my course; I have kept the faith. Henceforth there is laid up for me a crown of righteousness which the Lord, the righteous Judge, shall give me at that day." Finally, notice:

IV. The Anticipated Salvation

"For now is our salvation nearer than when we believed."

The people to whom Paul wrote these words were already in a state of salvation; but the end of their faith was their final salvation from all conflict, from all darkness, from all sin and from all sorrow. And such a state can be enjoyed only on the other side of the "river" — with Christ in Heaven. Not till then shall our warfare be over. Each breath we breathe, each step we take, brings us nearer to our heavenly Home. What does this salvation imply? One of Paul's sorrows on earth came through the buffetings of Satan and through the untiring evil of sin working in his members. This is the plague of our hearts, but soon we shall enter upon that glorious liberty of the children of God and shall be made perfect in holiness.

Sin is a darkness; but "there shall be no night there". Night shall be swallowed up in an everlasting day. There shall be no night of sorrow through temptation, fear or loneliness in that place where the Lamb, Who is the light thereof, shall wipe away all tears from their eyes. Neither shall they hunger any more, for He who is in the midst of the Throne shall feed them and lead them to living fountains of water. In His presence there is a fulness of joy, and at His right hand are pleasures for evermore. And we ought to live each day as if it were our last day here. We should always be ready; for we know not the hour when our Lord shall come. Have you ever noticed how those who are on a voyage across a sea stand in readiness to disembark when the harbour comes into view? Those who are going to the heavenly country may even now, by faith, view the desired haven and the fair shore of a better world. May he find us ready when He comes, with our lamps lit and our staff in our hand, and ready to disembark on the shore of that country wherein dwelleth righteousness.

But the night is far spent, the day is at hand. It may be that there are some listening to my voice who are moving toward a lost eternity. Is it not time you should leave the way of sin and return to God! Why should you die? "Behold, now is the day of salvation." Our earnest exhortation to you is— "Awake thou that sleepest, and arise from the dead and Christ shall give thee Light."

XI

" TILL THE END BE "

"But go thou thy way till the end be; for thou shalt rest, and stand in thy lot at the end of the days." (Dan. 12 : 13).

In these days we hear much about the subject of Christian consecration. All who belong to the Lord should, indeed, heed the exhortation: "Be ye holy, for I am holy." "Walk before me, and be thou perfect", was God's command to Abraham. It is also a command which is addressed to all the people of God in every age. Truly none of us is consecrated to the Lord to the degree that we should. This is our grief — or it should be. Though they cannot attain to perfection in this life the Lord's people, in the words of another, would be holy if they could. But one of their sorrows is that they are continually coming short of His glory.

Daniel, to whom these words were addressed by the Lord, was a man greatly devoted to His fear, His service and His glory. He enjoyed much of His secret. The Lord was also his Companion in the way. He therefore could say with the Psalmist: "Nevertheless I am continually with Thee." God speaks of him as a man "greatly beloved". The Lord loves all His people. They are all "greatly beloved"; but there are some who give clearer evidence in their lives that His love truly dwells in their hearts.

Although, as His prophet, the Lord revealed His mind to Daniel in so many things related to the future course of His Providence there were things which, in His infinite wisdom, He would not reveal. "It is the glory of God to conceal a thing." The Bible is an infallible revelation of God's mind and will; but His Providence is a great deep, the contents and unfoldings of which can only be understood with their fulfilment. "And I heard, but I understood not: then said I, O my Lord, what shall be the end of these things? And he said, Go thy way, Daniel, for the words are closed up and sealed till the time of the end." And in commanding him to go his way, the Lord leaves with him a great promise of eternal rest in Heaven where, "at the end of the days" he would also possess an unfading inheritance with Himself. These words — the command and the promise — are also addressed, and belong to all who truly love and fear His name. Let us consider:

I. The Divine Command

" But go thou thy way till the end be."

The implication of these words is that Daniel's way was wholly approved by God. God's way and that of His servant were identical. "The ways of the Lord are right, and the just shall walk in them."

When we look at this man's life as it is before us in this Book we may see how he walked before God. To begin with he walked consistently **in the way of Truth.** Both in his outward conduct and in his inward spiritual desires he was ruled by God's Word. God's will was pre-eminently his own. The prayer of David was inscribed on his heart also by the Holy Spirit:

"In Thy law's path make me to go,
For I delight therein."

He also could say, "Hold up my goings in Thy paths, that my footsteps slip not." When his enemies, for example, tried to ensnare him, the only fault they could find with him was that he refused to deviate from the law of his God. A higher testimonial than this was seldom given to any in this world. He would not grieve God's Spirit or cast a shadow on his own conscience by any compromise with evil. He would not adapt himself to the ways of a pagan and godless nation. Rather than deny the Truth of God in his worship and conduct, or go out of the way into any by-path of sin, he was prepared to die. His love to God and his devotion to His Word brought him into the den of lions. But the Guardian of Israel preserved his life there and made his enemies to see that there is a reward for the righteous. An old friend of mine used to remark that the night Daniel spent in the lion's den was the happiest he ever spent in this world. It passed all too quickly! In that lower cave God's blissful Presence filled his soul, while He was also a wall of fire round about him. God spread His covering wings over him, and no enemy in hell or on earth could touch him. If the way of Truth leads many of God's people into the way of suffering it is only that they might discover how great is His love, sympathy and faithfulness. To suffer for Christ is to be partaker of His own sufferings. And many of His people have discovered that in suffering for Him there is a joy no words can describe.

We notice also that the way of Truth is bound to **the way of holiness.** And in this way Daniel also walked. True holiness derives its power and complexion from the well of Truth. Our Lord in His great prayer of intercession emphasises this fact. "Sanctify them through the truth: Thy Word is Truth." "And an highway shall be there, and a way, and it shall be called The Way of Holiness: the unclean shall not pass over it, but it shall be for those: the wayfaring men, though fools, shall not err therein."

The Word of God everywhere enforces the truth that true holiness involves, on the one hand a life of separation, and on the other what we might call a life of proclamation, or a life of witness for God. In other words, holiness, in its outward manifestation, is both negative and positive. The Book of Psalms begins, for example, with a description of the happy or blessed man. "Blessed is the man that walketh not in the counsel of the ungodly, nor standeth in the way of sinners." When, in other days, Satan walked to and fro on the earth he saw one man who had no spiritual counterpart in his age. "And the Lord said unto Satan, Hast thou considered my servant Job, that there is none like him in the earth, a perfect and an upright man, one that feareth God and escheweth evil." Rather than defile their garments by following the evil course of this world, Daniel's young friends in the Lord chose to be cast into the furnace of fire. "Have no fellowship with the unfruitful works of darkness, but rather reprove them." Although we are in the world, we are not of the world. The so-called "good religious mixers" of this age who think they can serve God, while at the same time they crawl in the sewers of a sinful world, are far removed from this way. "Without holiness no man shall see the Lord" or dwell in His presence. Holiness is the very air which the inhabitants of the new Jerusalem breathe, "for there shall in no wise enter into it any thing that defileth neither whatsoever worketh abomination." True holiness is congenial only to the new man in Christ, while to the graceless man it is hateful and repugnant.

But holiness has also its positive side. It is not mere separation. It is a witnessing by our life and conversation whose we are and whom we serve. "Ye," said our Lord, "are the light of the World. A city that is set on an hill cannot be hid. Neither do men light a candle, and put it under a bushel, but on a candlestick, and it giveth light unto all that are in the house. Let your light so shine before men." Daniel was a man who, by his holy walk, shone like a lone star in the prevailing darkness.

There are two kinds of men and women within the visible Church in the world. There are those who take on the colour of the age in which they live. These walk with the times. And there are those whose path is "as the shining light, that shineth more and more unto the perfect day." These are they who have the promise that in the world to come they "shall shine as the

brightness of the firmament" and "as the stars for ever and ever".
The banner of truth and holiness has, therefore, its two sides. One
is a spiritual and moral separation from all ungodliness and the
other, personal witness that we are the children of the day.

We see that this man was also in **the way of prayer.** As holiness
derives its power from the fountain of Truth there is, on the other
hand, no spiritual growth or maturity without unceasing prayer.
We read of this man that three times each day he kneeled in
God's presence. He brought all his personal concerns to the Lord
at the Throne of Grace. But the great theme of his prayers was
the diminished state of God's cause. Israel — a people whom the
Lord had loved and embraced as His own — were in a state of
rebellion against Him. The nation was, therefore, under the rod
of His chastisement and indignation. The land was desolate. Its
lights were extinguished. The people were led into captivity. In
such "a day of rebuke and blasphemy" Daniel did not, however,
give way to despair. He continued to plead God's covenant
promises made to Abraham and to his seed.

It is good to know that as there is a continual intercession
going on "within the veil" for the Church by our great High
Priest, the Lord Jesus, there has not been an hour since the
beginning of time but the Lord had some on earth whose prayers
"like the pillars of smoke" have been ascending to Heaven. God's
people pray that Christ may prosper in His reign and kingdom
and that the enemies of His glory might be restrained. Whatever
discouragements and opposition they may meantime meet with
they "ought always to pray and not to faint". The exceeding
great and precious promises of God anticipate the coming day
when the question shall be asked once more, "who is she that
looketh forth as the morning, fair as the moon, clear as the sun,
and terrible as an army with banners?" The promises of God
and the prayers of His people are joined on this glorious issue.
They both anticipate the coming Day.

But is it not true that they are but few who are exercised in
this way, and who wrestle with God for the uplifting and revival
of His cause? Although, as in the days of Elisha, there might
have been many in Babylon who were secretly loyal to God and
His cause, they were not all like this man. May God give us the
grace to continue instant in prayer till He again pluck His hand
from His bosom and make known His saving power!

We notice also that although this man enjoyed such nearness
to God, He did not reveal to him the content, trials and conflicts
of his future life in this world. **The way of His Providence, as it
stood related to His servant, He kept a secret.** Nowhere do we see

the wisdom and the love of God so clearly as in this concealment. Were He to disclose to us beforehand the many sorrows which were to make up our cup in this life our hearts and lives would be crushed in apprehension and fear. He merely says, "Go thy way till the end be." And whatever may transpire in the way of His Providence He is ever beside His own to help and comfort them. "As thy days so shall thy strength be." This is His promise till the day dawn and the day star arise in our hearts. In His hand we are as safe as the saints in glory — though, as yet, not so happy. Let us also look at:

II. God's Promise

"For thou shalt rest and stand in thy lot at the end of the days."

The promise is two-fold. There is the promise of rest and the promise of possession. "There remaineth a rest to the people of God." This rest is going to be both perfect and eternal. Both our souls and our bodies are to participate in this sweet repose within the bosom of the Eternal. Already, as heirs of salvation, we have the beginnings of it in our heart, mind and conscience. It is a rest which is derived from our relationship and union with Christ. "We who have believed do enter unto rest." But not till we pass out of time shall we enjoy this rest in all its perfection and fulness.

We are to enjoy rest from sin and Satan. As in the case of Paul there is, in this life, a cry and a restlessness in the heart of all who know the Lord. Indwelling sin is tireless in its enmity to God's law which the new creature in Christ loves and which he would obey. David's cry was, "There is no rest in my bones because of my sin." And if sin is active in their members they are a people who also wage a constant warfare with Satan. "We wrestle not against flesh and blood, but against principalities and powers, against the rulers of the darkness of this world, against spiritual wickedness in high places." Sin and Satan are one in their opposition to all who would serve the Lord and obey His Word. Not until we cross the last river, and reach the end of our pilgrimage here, shall our warfare cease. The evil thoughts which so often terrify us, and the subtle temptations which so often cast their shadow over our spirits, shall one day be for ever removed. In eternity there shall be no room in our soul for sin or fear. God's presence and love shall wholly possess our beings. As the sun banishes the night so shall God's eternal day, with the unclouded dawn of the Sun of Righteousness, for ever remove every shadow of fear and sin. In heaven our souls shall be wholly possessed of God's love. Life's storms shall be changed into an everlasting calm.

We shall also rest from sorrow and sufferings. These shall for ever flee away. This promise is also given to those who labour for Christ — whether they labour for Him in secret or in public. **"They shall rest from their labours and their works do follow them."** And, however much the Lord's people may be discouraged in this life, in all their labours for Christ they shall know, in that day, that their labour in the Lord was not in vain. This rest shall be extended not only to the soul but to the body as well. It may be that your strength is now, through labour, age and infirmity, abated in the way. The once alert step is now reduced to a slow, uncertain pace. "The grasshopper" is becoming a burden. Signs are present with some of us that the earthly tabernacle is soon to be dissolved, and that we must soon lie down not to arise till the earth be no more. The rest of the body in the grave coincides with the rest of the soul in the mansions above. The two separate to meet again on the resurrection morning when the Lord shall come to awake His loved ones out of sleep. Sometimes we fear the approach of the last enemy, but Christ by His own death has rendered death harmless to His own people. And the Lord, Who rested in the grave, has warmed this bed for His loved ones. Our bodies are united to Him in the grave and when, at the sound of His voice, we awake we shall be satisfied with His likeness.

> I will both lay me down in peace
> And quiet sleep will take;
> Because Thou only me to dwell
> In safety, Lord, dost make.

But there is also **the Promise of Possession.** "Thou shalt stand in thy lot at the end of the days." Before He ascended into Heaven our Lord comforted His people by assuring them that He was going away to prepare a place for them in a better world. "Ye are they who have continued with me in my temptations", and "I go to prepare a kingdom for you" — a kingdom "which is incorruptible and undefiled and that fadeth not away". Beyond what is revealed it would be presumptuous on our part to seek to describe what heaven is like. There are, indeed, no words in our earthly vocabulary which could do justice to this theme. "Eye hath not seen, nor ear heard, neither have entered into the heart of men the things which God hath prepared for them that love Him. But God hath revealed them to us by His Spirit." But the glory and the happiness of Heaven are derived from Christ. "The Lamb is the light thereof." He is the Tree of Life. The wellsprings of the redeemed are wholly in Him. It is the fulness of His love, enjoyed by all His people, that shall move their lips to praise

Him. The supreme joy of Heaven, therefore, is not **the place but the Person** of our full enjoyment of God. Only God can justify the renewed soul. He is the inheritance and lot of all His people. How well does the Psalmist express this:

"God is of mine inheritance,
and cup the portion:
The lot that fallen is to me
Thou dost maintain alone.

Unto me happily the lines
in pleasant places fell;
Yea, the inheritance I got
in beauty doth excel."

John Duncan used to say in his latter years that his very soul was woven, in an ever deepening desire, into the words— "to enjoy Him for ever". Many a sad day the believer has in this life; but O, the promise of the Beloved which shall have its fulfilment when our nights of weeping shall be no more. "Sorrow and sighing shall flee away."

And think of how they are to stand before God in their inheritance. All their happiness, all their possessions, are eternally secure through the righteousness of their unchangeable Redeemer in which they stand before God. "He hath dispersed abroad, he hath given to the poor. His righteousness remaineth for ever."

We come into this, our lot, "at the end of the days". Our days and nights here pass as a tale that is told, but the end of these shall mark the dawn of our eternal day when our sun shall no more go down. "For there shall be no night there."

Meantime let us pray for the needed grace that shall enable us to go from strength to strength until we appear before God in Zion.

There may be those among us who move, without concern, in the broad way which leads to destruction. To all such God speaks, "Turn ye, turn ye . . . why will ye die?" The way of life begins with our reconciliation to God through the blood of Christ. The way out of the kingdom of darkness into the path of life begins with the blood of sprinkling, through beholding and receiving the "Lamb of God who taketh away the sin of the world." "Who is wise and he shall understand these things ? prudent, and he shall know them ? for the ways of the Lord are right, and the just shall walk in them; but the transgressors shall fall therein ! " O! may we all meet at His right hand where there are pleasures for evermore. Pray, dear soul, that yours may not be an eternal night, but an eternal day, with Christ The Day Star in your heart. May the Lord bless His own Word.

XII

THE SOUL'S COMPASSION

"We are journeying into the place of which the Lord said, I will give it you: come thou with us, and we will do thee good: for the Lord hath spoken good concerning Israel." (Numbers 10 : 29).

In the lives of most men and women there are moments when they are presented with solemn issues which may profoundly affect their future lives, if not their destiny. This is especially true of those who hear the Gospel. Such solemn issues call for careful and prayerful consideration, and by the grace of God, for a wise decision. A wrong decision, or no decision at all, may involve us in regret, in remorse, and in everlasting sorrow. On the other hand, a right response to the overtures of God in the Gospel shall bring us into the way of peace and eternal happiness.

In this chapter we read of a man who, at the cross-roads of destiny, was asked by Moses to throw in his lot with the people of God. He was also given the promise that if he did so, he would truly share in their blessings and in their inheritance. We have reason to believe that although Hobab at first hesitated in obeying the word which God through His servant addressed to him, he did join himself to the Israel of God and that he became an heir of the righteousness which is of faith. And because, I believe, there are in this congregation some, if not many, to whom this appeal is also addressed by God in His Word I want to give these solemn words a personal application.

Hobab, we believe, is with God in heaven, but you may be here still "halting between two opinions", with eternity very near, and your precious soul unsaved and your time unredeemed. Although you are still in the room of mercy, do remember that you may yet be a stranger to God. Your state, therefore, is truly perilous. Let us offer a few remarks on these words.

Let us consider:

1. **The Urgent Appeal and The Loving Invitation**

"Come thou with us."

Hobab, we know, was related to Moses by natural bonds; but it was not any mere natural affection which lay behind these words of Moses. True, the Lord's people, like Paul, have a concern for those who are their kinsmen according to the flesh; but their spiritual concern, prayers and affections go beyond their own immediate circles. They would, indeed, have all men come to the knowledge of the Truth and of Christ. In this matter they are also, like Paul, constrained by the love of Christ. Christ Himself has compassion on the ignorant and on those who are out of the way. On earth He wept over those who, in their folly, moved toward eternal destruction, but whom He would have gathered under His wings. If we have a measure of the spirit of Christ **our** compassion also will go out to the wayward and the lost. Who can remain silent before God as they see the great harvest which might be reaped for Him if true labourers were on the scene! If we were the means of bringing even one soul to seek salvation how great would be our joy in the day of Christ! In the words of Samuel Rutherford, heaven would be heaven twice over if, in the world of glory, we saw one who came to Christ as the result of our prayers or of our witness.

If, like Moses, we belong to Christ, we would have others share our spiritual happiness. Moses, in the midst of all his afflictions, was a happy man. So were God's true Israel whom the Lord had saved, not from mere temporal danger, but from the power and consequence of sin. "Happy art thou, O Israel, O people saved by the Lord." The day he and they came to the knowledge of God, and had tasted that He was merciful and gracious, was the day when they found the key to everlasting blessedness. "O, taste and see that God is good." Only God is good. Only God alone can give us the desire of our heart. "This," said David, in speaking of his hope of enjoying eternal communion with God, "is all my salvation and this is all my desire."

Moses, as we know, was offered the best — or the worst — that this world could give him. He was, perhaps, even offered a throne. He was offered all the pleasures, all the riches and all the honours that this world could confer upon him. Not merely some of these earthly and carnal favours, but all of them. But when he tasted of the heavenly life, and of the deep unspeakable enjoyment of communion with God, he, as an immortal being, knew how empty and vain were all created things. He knew that earthly "things" are ultimately irrelevant to such as are destined to exist for ever. He knew that man can carry nothing with him to eternity but either sin or God. God had forgiven him his sin, and had made him an heir of glory. He knew that to live in sin and to be deprived of God's mercy and love would involve him in misery and despair for ever and ever. O, my dear fellow sinner, we are not trying to deceive you when we say with him, "Come thou with us, and we will do thee good." "How great is thy goodness, which thou hast laid up for them that fear thee: which thou hast wrought for them that trust in thee before the sons of men!" God's people only enjoy an earnest, or a foretaste, here of what is awaiting them in the world to come, but even these drops from heaven are infinitely preferable to all the so-called joys which this unclean and empty world can bestow.

Let me say something else. Paul, you will remember, speaks of the "terror of the Lord". And knowing what that meant he sought to persuade men to "flee from the wrath to come". Moses also knew what these words meant. He extended his earnest invitation to Hobab because he knew that the alternative to God's goodness and obedience to His will would be His eternal displeasure. He had seen with his own eyes the dire consequences of disobeying God's voice and of living a shelterless life outwith the safety which Christ's death and blood provide. He saw the land of Egypt come under God's anger and become a veritable city of destruction. The deluge of wrath which descended on Egypt and of which he was a witness was, however, limited and momentary. But "the wrath to come" is unmixed with mercy and is eternal. And since it is the will of God that none should perish but that all should return to Him and live, this precious invitation is not merely from man's heart or lips but from the heart of God Himself. We are but Christ's ambassadors who plead with men to be reconciled to God.

The blessed implication of these words, you will notice, is that the free offer of salvation and the invitations of the Gospel have the sanction of God's Word. We find them in every part of Scripture. Our Lord addressed men in these words: "Come unto me, all ye that labour and are heavy laden, and I will give you rest." Since all men enter the world under a burden of guilt and sin these words are, therefore, addressed to "all". None is excluded. One of the last words in the Bible is "Come". The Spirit and the bride say "Come". The Church unites in uttering the same word as Christ and the Spirit. So do all who hear and obey God's voice.

To say that this appeal to men implies that they have some measure of ability to save themselves is not true. In the matter of salvation man, of himself, can do nothing. He is utterly helpless. But there are, on the other hand, three solemn facts which confront us in relation to the offer and invitations of the Gospel. The first is that man is accountable to God. Why shall the ungodly be excluded on the last day from the presence of God? Is it because they had lost all ability to come to Christ? No. "I was a stranger and you took me not in." He knocked at their door, but they kept it closed. How often, and in how many ways, has He knocked at your own?

Another truth is that there is something we can do. This is not a contradiction of what we have just said. We can pray. We can cry for mercy. "I waited patiently for the Lord, and He inclined unto me and heard my cry." It is truly God's power and hand that rescues us from the pit of sin; but, as in the case of the Psalmist, He does this in answer to prayer. Prayer is always the expression of our inability to save ourselves. You stay as you are and you will remain where you are. Keep silent and God may keep silent also. The cry of a drowning man cannot save him, but it may bring someone to his side who can rescue him. Let me ask the Lord's people here this question. Was it not in answer to prayer, and with your eye upon Christ crucified, that the Lord saved you? I can almost hear the still small voice of a universal "yea" within the souls of all to whom the question comes.

There is another and a more important truth which we should mention. When Moses said to Hobab, "Come thou with us", the Holy Spirit accompanied that word to his heart and made him willing in a day of His power. The Holy Spirit, who is present in His own infallible Word, is He who quickens us and who draws the soul to Christ. Here, then, is a mystery of God's sovereignty which is beyond our comprehension. "The wind," said Christ, "bloweth where it listeth, and thou hearest the sound thereof but canst not tell whence it cometh, and whither it goeth: so is every one that is born of the Spirit." May that blessed wind, from the very portals of heaven, waft into your soul and bear you away to the very place whence it has its rise. When, therefore, we say, "Come thou with us", we do so in the hope that the blessed Spirit who also says "Come" may, through our words, work effectively in your heart.

Sometimes when we speak to men and women about their need of salvation, and of their duty to come to Christ, they reply that they are, as yet, "not good enough". But, as one put it, Christ did not come to save little sinners or good sinners, but great sinners and bad sinners. Christ saved the poor publican who cried for mercy while He left the proud and "good" Pharisee severely alone. How unspeakably solemn and terrible is the divine contempt in relation to such men who put their own righteousness before Christ's. We are all in the same category. Our best, before God, is often our worst; for we substitute our own imperfect and soiled righteousness for the spotless righteousness of Christ. My dear fellow sinner, be not deceived. He wants you as you are. There is no sin in your heart or in your life but His blood can wash away. Our God is a forgiving God. "Who is a God like unto Thee that pardoneth iniquity and passeth by the transgression of the remnant of his heritage? He retaineth not his anger for ever, because he delighteth in mercy." Let me say, like many another who obtained mercy, that there was a dark distressing season in my own life when a deep fear lurked in my heart that I had a sin, in the shape of evil thoughts, which God would not and could not forgive. But when He passed by me in mercy, and spoke to my soul in love I saw the wonder of His forgiveness, and the depth of pity which is in His Being toward the lost. "Come thou with us", and you will discover this for yourself.

Look again at:

II. The Sure Hope and The Great Promise:

Moses assured Hobab that they were "journeying to the place of which the Lord said, I will give it you", and that He had "spoken good concerning Israel". God had, indeed, promised His people that He would bring them into a land flowing with milk and honey. We know also that because of their unbelief and disobedience many in that camp never saw that good land. Moses himself was denied that favour. He saw the good land from the top of Pisgah, but, literally speaking, he did not inhabit it. He was already in Heaven when he appeared on another mount — the Mount of Transfiguration — talking to the Lord.

It is good to know that Canaan was but a type of that other land "which is fairer than day" — the heavenly country. The natural Canaan was but a pale imperfect shadow of Heaven. While Moses, therefore, might have included the lower Canaan in his words to Hobab, we know that his eyes and heart were fixed on "Him Who is invisible" and on the place where He dwells. This was how he endured amid all the tribulations of his life. In the Epistle to the Hebrews Moses, and all the heirs of God's promises, are spoken of as spiritual men who desired and sought that country wherein dwelleth righteousness. They saw spiritual and eternal realities by faith. God and Heaven were more real to them than this sinful world which is, after all, but a passing shadow. As spiritual men they had put this world for ever behind their back. They had become pilgrims and strangers on the earth. This then is what Moses truly meant when he said, "We are journeying to the place of which the Lord said, "I will give it you". They were journeying to the new Jerusalem which is from above.

And those who are going to Heaven are in the way to Heaven. How will you reach your own home after this service? Only by taking the right way to your own door. And unless you are in the way to Heaven how can you reach it?

For Moses and his people this journey began with the slaying of the paschal lamb and "the blood of sprinkling". "When I see the blood I will pass over you". This transaction was typical of the great atonement which Christ made for the redemption of His people. He is the way to Heaven. "I am the way and the truth and the life". It is through His merits and death that we have access to God, and are provided with a way of escape out of our bondage. It is through His death that God's saving power operates for our salvation. It was through the blood of sprinkling that God's arm was outstretched to make a pathway for His people through the deep.

Another evidence that they were in God's way was that God provided for their daily needs. Hobab might have wondered how the great host who were journeying through the wilderness could survive the journey. But he came to know that this favoured people had a daily supply of manna from Heaven, and that a stream from the rock followed them to the end. Dear friend, who may be still ignorant of the blessings which God's people enjoy, little do you know of their enjoyments. They feed on Christ, the "bread of life". They drink daily from the river of life which flows from the smitten "Rock of Ages". Goodness and mercy shall follow them all the days of their life here. Their bread shall be given them, and their water shall be sure. But till you come with us, you shall know nothing of the spiritual fare which nourishes the souls of His people. He has prepared this table for them in the wilderness. "They go from strength to strength, every one of them in Zion appeareth before God." "Eye hath not seen, nor ear heard, neither have entered in the heart of man the things which God has prepared for them that love Him: but God hath revealed them unto us by His Spirit."

To enjoy the rest and the happiness which remain for the people of God, Hobab must also share in their afflictions. Israel was surrounded by enemies. Their souls were often discouraged because of the way. But afflictions are not hostile to our true happiness or to our holiness. Very often our greatest blessings come through our greatest trials. Besides, the true believer has more joy in his afflictions, both actually and prospectively, than graceless men have in all their choice pleasures. Their sighs and tears are preferable to the smiles and frivolities of the ungodly. The greatest honour and privilege that can be conferred on us here is that we should be partakers of Christ's sufferings. If we are in the way of Heaven we shall reach the desired haven through many storms. Moses did not conceal or exclude this fact when he spoke to Hobab. Do we participate in the trials of His people? Are we in the footsteps of His flock? If so, we are journeying to the place where sorrow is unknown.

The greatest happiness that Moses knew on earth was the enjoyment of God's presence. This was not personal or exclusive to Himself. The Lord was also in the midst of His people. He dwelt between the cherubims in the most holy place. The pillar of cloud by day and of fire by night was over the camp always. It was not only the symbol of His gracious presence, but also of His nearness and protecting power. What solemnity, sweetness and comfort did this lend to the hearts of His people! "Lo, I am with you always." "My presence shall go with you and I will give you rest." You, who have enjoyed moments, hours or days of God's presence in your own soul, know that this verily is Heaven in the foretaste. Short of this, we have nothing. Without this we shall have nothing but utter desolation for ever. To know God in His love and gracious Presence reduces all other favours to mere nothingness. My dear fellow sinner, when we say to you, "Come thou with us and we will do you good", it is not something of our own that we want to impart to you, but to know Christ "whom to know is life eternal". This is the great goodness to which you also are invited.

By the words, "We will do thee good", was Moses not also emphasising how wonderful is the communion of the saints on earth, and that we are safer and happier in the company of God's people than in the company of those who know not God? The Lord warns us in His Word that the companions of fools shall be destroyed. Ruth, by choosing the people of God as her companions, is now in Heaven. So is David who said, "I am a companion of all those who fear thee." Dear Christless friend, we are not perfect. Far from it. God's people have their own infirmities and failings. They are still in the flesh. If you go about with your magnifying glass you will find spots and flaws in their life. Like Paul, they all acknowledge themselves to be the chief of sinners. But those who belong to God have something which you will never find elsewhere. You have even now a place in their affections, in their prayers, and in their desire for your salvation. O, how happy would the Lord's people here tonight be if you also would say with Ruth: "Entreat me not to leave thee, or to return from following after thee; for whither thou goest I will go, and where thou lodgest I will lodge; thy people shall be my people and thy God my God."

In conclusion, let me say a word on:

III. His Hesitation and Decision

As we have remarked, Hobab's immediate reaction to Moses' appeal was unfavourable. As he viewed the present state of Israel, and compared it to his own temporal comforts, he was inclined to reject his offer. Israel was a people apparently homeless. They were moving within the heart of a barren and dreary land. Their past afflictions were many. Their future trials might be even greater. He had an earthly home of his own. He lived among a people who cared for his temporal welfare. He lacked nothing in God's providence. But something happened. Yes, something happened. Moses' second appeal moved his heart to go with him. Perhaps, at that moment, he also had a glimpse and a foretaste of the things which are unseen and eternal. The Holy Spirit unveiled his inner eyes and enabled him to taste and see something of the great goodness laid up in heaven for all who fear God and follow Him. In Joshua, Chapter Four, we have Hobab's name and some of his descendants mentioned as being members of God's Israel. Hobab therefore did "come". O! that this would happen to you.

The Lord's people should persevere in prayer and persuasion where precious souls are concerned. We must never conceal from them the worth of our inheritance, and the certainty of its possession. Our prayers, our words and invitations God may bless in their salvation. Even a casual word of welcome and exhortation to Christless souls may be the means of arresting them in their sinful ways. All Christians have a lovely story to tell and a lovely Saviour to commend. They are on the way to a lovely place which is their eternal Home. The gates into this blessed Home are open night and day to all who would enter in.

Notice also how Moses detected in this man latent gifts and talents which the Lord might, by His grace, use for the good of His cause in this world. How unspeakably sad it is to see men of gifts and parts serving the world and the enemy of their souls! Only a few days ago have I listened to two young men preaching the good tidings of salvation. Like Hobab they once hesitated, but now they know the joy of the Lord and they display the banner of Truth and fight His battles. Are you here, either misusing or burying your talents? Great, dear friend, will be your sorrow and remorse in eternity if you do not give your Creator His own back with its interest. Remember, the night is coming when no man shall be able to work. Your opportunity and your day of grace are passing away. "Jesus of Nazareth passeth by."

Moses was moving on when he met Hobab. And your present privilege may never be repeated. We, also, say to you from the depths of our heart: "Come thou with us and we will do thee good." Will you, like Mary, make choice of Christ, the Good Part? Will you, like this man of old, be one of His in the day when He shall make up His Jewels? Will you, whether old or young, be among those who shall praise Him in His Zion? "Acquaint now thyself with Him and be at peace: thereby good shall come unto thee."